QUICKSAND *Tales*

'Reading this book feels like being drawn into the confidence of a hapless friend ... Vibrant and entertaining, sure to inspire a healthy dose of schadenfreude in its readers'
Irish Times

'I loved it. Keggie is chaos in motion, yearning for everything to go right and, luckily for us, it rarely does. She has a wonderfully sharp eye for character, draws every scene so vividly and it's funny, witty. Never arch. Funny. And awful'
ROBERT BATHURST

'Charming ... Carew has a beautifully evocative style'
Evening Standard

'Carew has a knack for spinning an amusing yarn, and this account of her life's various disasters can be painfully funny'
Herald

'Delicately and deftly told, *Quicksand Tales* reads like a collection of carefully crafted short stories, infused with the added truth of being taken from Carew's own extraordinary experiences'
Salisbury Journal

Also by Keggie Carew

Dadland

QUICKSAND
Tales

The Misadventures of
KEGGIE
CAREW

CANONGATE

This paperback edition published in Great Britain, the USA and Canada in 2020
by Canongate Books

First published in Great Britain, the USA and Canada in 2019
by Canongate Books Ltd, 14 High Street, Edinburgh EH1 1TE

Distributed in the USA by Publishers Group West
and in Canada by Publishers Group Canada

canongate.co.uk

1

British Library Cataloguing-in-Publication Data
A catalogue record for this book is available on
request from the British Library

ISBN 978 1 78689 408 3

Typeset in Bembo by Palimpsest Book Production Ltd,
Falkirk, Stirlingshire

Printed and bound in Great Britain by Clays Ltd, Elcograf S.p.A.

For Jonathan

CONTENTS

PREFACE

I have had my fair share of awkward predicaments and the toe-curling mortification of the aftermath. Something irresistible attracts mishap and misadventure to me, or me to it. I effortlessly put my foot in it. Say the wrong thing, do the wrong thing. Yet for someone with few qualms about not conforming, why, oh why, is my internal discomfort so deep? If fate is not conspiring against me, then it must be something to do with me.

I feel an affinity with people who have excruciating things happen to them. Obviously they make me feel better, but there is something beautifully levelling about it too. Picasso said a picture hung crookedly on a wall tells you a lot more about the owner than a straight one ever could; he preferred crooked pictures. He knew, of course, we are all crooked pictures, busy in the lifelong pursuit of straightening ourselves, yet it is the straight picture we strive to portray.

The crack that yawns open to swallow us is the place that interests me. Making a hash of it. Being human. The tripwires of our hasty conclusions, our fixed ideas, our contradictions in thinking, our tribal prejudices, our base selves. As witness to my own prosecution I am forced to inspect the soft underbelly of my unruly, conflicted self. Not for absolution, but to embrace the human drama. To let the air out.

In the years of working away in the quiet anonymity of my shed I have often been encouraged by writers' aphorisms, by their tips and guidance, by their *bons mots*. Muriel Spark's advice: 'You are writing a letter to a friend . . . Write privately, not publicly; without fear or timidity, right to the end of the letter, as if it was never going to be published'. Or as the poet Liz Lochhead said, 'You are stuck with something until the point where you go, "To hell with it, I'll tell the truth."'

The stories in this book are true. Some contain privacy-protection mechanisms, but they are all strictly faithful to my experience of what occurred. I am obsessively superstitious about it. Tamper with the evidence and the human reaction and outcome will be altered, the truth lost or perverted. And truth has to take priority over finer feelings. It is rarely comfortable. But that is life. I laughed when Colm Tóibín on *Desert Island Discs* refuted the idea of waiting until someone had died to tell a story. His solution was to ring them up and say, 'You know that awful story you told me last week with all those personal details in it, well, I've written it up and it's being published next week!'

Any good story, for me, has disaster in there somewhere. So I began to collect mine. In some I am the witless protagonist, in others a reluctant witness or victim of circumstance, but I am always there – in the silent groan. Alarmingly, the pile on my desk is still growing. The earliest story in this collection happened on the eve of my twentieth birthday, yet every detail remains as chilling as if it happened yesterday; the most recent is too recent for comfort. These are not banana-skin tales, but more my mother's medicine – gallows humour. Human fuck-ups. Mostly mine, but not always . . . Perfect storms, incompetence, paranoia, insecurity, clumsiness, privileged lives and over-fed white middle-class anxieties, dark deeds or pure bad luck at being in the wrong place at the wrong time. Some are just terrible. Some are not terrible at all, just excruciating. Anything that makes me shudder gets an airing. When the mirror throws back that bright, bitter shame; when good intentions fall short in our unequal world. I am recycling awfulness.

Flawed creatures that we are, I hope these voyages into quicksand might lessen our shared fragility.

Keggie Carew, 2019

'Fail again. Fail better.'
SB

'Fail again. Fail worse.'
KC

THE LATE VISITOR

It is 1976. The year of the Entebbe hijack, of the IRA bombings in London, of the first commercial Concorde flight, of *Taxi Driver* and *M*A*S*H*. Liberal party leader Jeremy Thorpe is accused of hiring a hitman to murder his homosexual lover. Jimmy Carter moves into the White House. It has been a scorching summer. I'm nineteen, and life at home has been terrible; Dad has left, Mum is ill, my sister, Nicky, and I have gone feral living off jam sandwiches. I've bunked off school, done badly in my A levels, my boyfriend has gone to university but I know I have no chance with my lousy grades. I have been working as a barmaid and making clay necklaces, and have saved enough money to buy a one-way ticket to Toronto. The only reason I have chosen Toronto is because I met some Canadians in the pub I was working in, so I have an address where I can stay for a few days, which makes the leap a little less daunting.

So off I go on my beginning-to-regret-I-ever-mentioned-it adventure, wearing my Doc Marten boots, with everything I think I need in my dad's WW2 army backpack with its ridiculously uncomfortable metal waistband and heavy leather straps.

I

When I arrive in Toronto at the end of October it is already bitterly cold. I have never felt cold like it, a whistling-through-you cold that my thin brown coat and gappy knitted jumper do nothing to allay. After a week of trudging around on my own – for my Canadian friends are busy at work – I catch a bus south to Hamilton to meet an English friend, Ian. I cannot remember what he was doing in Hamilton, but we decide to head south into the United States, and because we have very little money we hitch-hike. We take a route through the backwater states of Ohio, Kentucky, Missouri, Arkansas, and it is quite eventful, but miraculously we survive, and get rides all the way to Texas. In Texas I notice a large billboard on the side of the freeway advertising horse-riding trips with pictures of cowboys lassoing cattle, and on a whim we decide to check it out because I have always wanted to ride western style like a cowboy, so we ask our ride to drop us off the interstate at the next junction, which is a place called Sweetwater. Sweetwater is right in the heart of Texas, almost dead centre in fact; it is a flattish town with wide streets and low houses, and while we can't find any cowboys lassoing cattle, it is big on cotton, oil and rattlesnakes. Which is exotic enough to make us stay and try to find jobs. We are conspicuous with our packs and because we are the only two people who go around town on foot. There are no pavements on these wide streets which seem to be made only for big cars with big noses that sort of bound and glide everywhere, even in and out of the take-away. For me it is like being in an American movie. We ask around if there is any work and are directed to the local cotton gin (where raw cotton is processed); and there we are hired by a bemused Texan foreman wearing a cream Stetson hat to work with the Mexican 'wetbacks' – illegal workers (of whom we were two) – so called after the migrants who had to swim the Rio Grande to get across the US border. Our job is to shift and stack massive 600lb bales of cotton with a large cotton bale hook called a gaucho – there's a knack. Not the best at this, I graduate to driving the forklift in the warehouse, where I shine and show off as the fastest driver and most accurate cotton-bale stacker in the whole gin – an accolade bemusedly conceded by cowboys and Mexicans alike. We are earning $2 an hour with time-and-a-half overtime, and working 90 hours a week, give or take an hour, so our take-home pay is around $230 a week (the equivalent of more than a thousand dollars today), which for a nineteen-year-old in 1976 is a *whopping* amount. I'm certainly earning more than my dad is back in Britain, where an average wage for a man is less than £70 a week (£45 for a woman). What's more, at night I double it with a preposterous streak of beginner's luck at pool in a pool hall downtown called The Green Room, where there is an endless supply of cowboys ready to put their money down on the table and take me on.

We work, play pool and save money. We buy a black VW Beetle and call it Horace – you give names to cars when you're nineteen. The plan is to drive to South America, so we convert it into a camping Beetle that we can sleep in. We take the back seats out – this is in the days when the seats were on runners which you could just undo and pull the seats right out. For sleeping, we rig up a system where you slide out the front seats and flip them so the backrest is horizontal on the floor and the seat is wedged vertically against the front dash. Then we jigsaw out a 3-ply board which fits into the back with a hinged section that folds over into the front when the seats are turned round, which basically turns the whole car into a double bed. I make some foam cushions for a mattress, put up some curtains in a Navajo fabric with a zig-zaggy geometric design, with enough left over to cover the ceiling. It is homey. On the outside we paint a wide white stripe right over the top, across the roof, bonnet and boot, to reflect the heat we are expecting in the tropics. It is a very distinctive car. It looks like a skunk.

By early spring we have worked so many hours and played so many games of pool that we have saved a fortune, so we give in our notice. We want to see some more of the States before we head south, so we drive to Tombstone and the Grand Canyon and the Painted Desert, into California and Yosemite, Big Sur, San Francisco, Death Valley. We free-camp to save money, and anyway the season hasn't started so no parks are open until May.

On 21 April 1977, late in the afternoon, we arrive at Lake Tahoe in California looking for a place to camp. Lake Tahoe is a big blue lake and a well-known beauty spot surrounded by pine forests in which you are allowed to picnic, but not until May. We drive off the road, ignoring the 'No Camping' sign, and into the forest. The ground is hard and dry and we slowly putt along through the trees. We need to drive quite a way in order not to be seen and thrown off by park rangers, so we continue until we are well out of sight and sound of the road. We choose a nice flat picnic spot with a table and BBQ provided (these civilised Americans). We set Horace up for sleeping, slide out and flip up the front seats, make up the bed, collect firewood. We are delighted with our fine secluded spot. However, we have hardly been there an hour when a grizzled old-timer with some pots and pans turns up. He tells us he's a gold-panner. We talk a little, have a cup of tea, but interesting as a gold-panner is, this particular night neither of us are in the mood for an uninvited supper guest, because we've splashed out and have got two steaks lined up. I'm not unfriendly but slowly become more monosyllabic until he eventually slopes off, pans rattling as he goes. We get the BBQ going. Wrap a couple of potatoes in foil and nudge them into the embers, boil up some carrots, sizzle the steaks, which give off a mouth-watering aroma. Stars come out. The treetop silhouettes are spiky black against the velvet sky. We eat our delicious supper. Sit by the crackling fire. Everything is perfect.

Out of nowhere another figure comes out of the forest. He is standing in front of us. A very big guy. With a sack. He puts the sack on the picnic table as if he's staking a claim. He must be six foot four or five, he has a short crew cut and he wears an open-neck camouflage shirt with khaki pants. He wants food. We scrabble around and he eats everything we can find. He eats the biscuits and the bread and the one leftover burnt potato in the foil, and the cheese and the bar of chocolate. Then he picks up Ian's knife. A large, sharp, steel, wooden-handled knife we used mostly for chopping carrots. And he plays with it. Rubbing the blade against his thumb. I am now wishing I hadn't given the gold-panner the cold shoulder. I try to engage our visitor in conversation. I ask him his name. He says 'Animal'. It's not a good start. Ian asks him what he does. He's a mercenary. Just back from Angola, he adds. In the news a few months previously, three mercenaries had been executed by firing squad in Angola. Two Britons and an American. I stupidly mention this. I hear the words blurting childishly out before I can retrieve them. Trying to be friends, trying to make everything normal. He says the American was his brother. Still playing with the knife, he tells us that as a young boy, brought up by the Navajo, he'd been taught survival and how to live in the wild. He can track anything, he says, kill a bear with his bare hands, run fast as a deer, sleep with one eye open and one eye shut. He shows us the bullet holes in his biceps and the scars on his chest – describing how he got each one (people or animals 'messing with him'). Then he goes over to Horace, bends down, puts both hands under the front door and lifts one side right off the ground, so the car is suspended on two wheels. We laugh nervously.

Animal says he was in Vietnam and begins to explain in great detail how they tortured the Viet Cong for information. One method he describes was to heat up a metal pipe until it was red hot, then plunge it into their stomachs and haul out their guts. He smiles grimly. Then with a swift lunge he grabs my hand and thrusts it in the fire and pulls it out again. Ha! he laughs. After Vietnam he worked as a contract killer. Well, we did ask. He tells us how each hitman leaves their special mark, and that if he killed us, for instance, only his colleagues in the trade would know – from the information in their special reports – by his signature marks on our bodies. Where most hitmen take the ear of their victim to send back, Animal prefers to take the scalp. A nod to his Navajo foster parents, apparently.

In demonstration, he stands behind me, grabs a fistful of my hair and, while holding it up, marks little notches three inches apart around my head with the tip of the knife. The nicks are tiny but enough for me to feel each prick and the faintest trickle of blood. Just a joke, just a little fun, ha, ha. He is holding my hair tight, twisting the spray slightly, tauntingly, daring me to protest. Ian looks on uncomfortably. Neither of us know what on earth to do, because as Animal is demonstrating his scalping technique, he is also telling us that if anyone crosses him he will hunt them down and find them wherever they are, whatever country they are in. He eyeballs Ian sharply.

By now it is midnight. The embers of the fire are glowing, fading, glowing, fading. More stars have come out. On the outside I am managing to stay calm and cool, but on the inside my temperature has dropped ten degrees. My voice is not shaky, but measured and congenial, as if I am his friend, as if I trust that he is our friend, but inside I am terrified. My mind is flying around trying to think how we can escape. With the bed set up and seats flipped round, the car is undrivable. Animal could out-run us both. And I can't think of anything. And I can't believe that I can't, because I always thought that if I was ever in a compromising situation I would come up with something, and now that I am being tested, I am empty. I am completely blank. The one thing that seems vital is to act like there is nothing to worry about, that all this is normal. That we are just having a friendly chat. That no harm is meant. Animal is just throwing his weight about a bit.

He is now gouging out great chunks of the National Park picnic table with our knife: A. N. I. Maybe I *am* imagining it. M. A . . . Maybe this is just an American tough-guy kind of thing, maybe Ian is not worried and understands the situation better than I do, or maybe I am just spooked. L. He blows away the splinters. I tell Animal it is my mother's birthday the next day – which it is, April 22 – and I need to call her, and because of the time difference, I have to call early, so I need to go to bed. Then I add, possibly a little too pointedly, that she is *expecting* my call. Animal says I will be getting up a lot earlier than I'd planned, and that 'Ma' might not be getting her call. The first direct threat, indirectly . . .

If we didn't know before, we know now that we are in a very perilous position. This guy is a time bomb. Anything might set him off. Either he is all that he says he is: a killer psychopath and a very dangerous man; or he is a nutter – a very big, strong and imaginative one – and a very dangerous man. Either way, we are in the shit.

I can see Animal's demeanour has changed. He orders us to get into the car. He is going to sleep, he tells us, with his back leaning up against the driver's door. We get into Horace. Animal is four inches away. And it is now, at the moment when I shut the car door and Animal is out of sight, that I lose my outwardly cool appearance. My fear takes on a visceral reaction that overwhelms my whole body. I start to shake uncontrollably. My hair follicles actually stand on end. I can feel them. My shaking is making the car shake. This terrifies me more because I think he might think we are up to something, or canoodling, or worse, which might infuriate him and send him into a rage. And I glance at Ian, vainly hoping I am imagining this and that he – far more worldly than me – is not scared at all, but a white look flashes between us and I know. We are lying down – for that is all we can do – and I am shaking, looking up at the Navajo zig-zaggy fabric on the ceiling, thinking I'm not going to make my twentieth birthday, just two days away. Thinking: what *does* one think if one only has a few hours left? And then trying to think it. Trying to think of my family, my dad and my mum, my sister and brothers. But not sure what to think about them. I am mouthing in my head: I love you, Dad; I love you, Mum; I love you Patrick and Nicky and Tim. And I am trying to think about my family, and have good thoughts. But Ian is trying to talk to me, which makes me even more scared, as I am sure Animal can hear everything with his supersonic hearing, so I put my hand over Ian's mouth to try and stop him. But he pulls my hand away, and eventually he manages to whisper a plan in my ear.

I am to get out of the car with the torch, tell Animal I need a pee, walk into the woods, stop, turn the torch off, then run as fast as I can and get to the road, where Ian will meet me, once he's told Animal that I've gone. The theory behind the plan is that Animal will not think I will run off on my own, leaving Ian, and so he will allow me to go for a pee. Once I am free, however, he will know that I will be able to identify him, which hopefully will discourage him from harming Ian. It is not perfect, but it is all we have. I am amazed that Ian has the steeliness to come up with a plan in the first place, and doubly astonished he is brave enough to remain with Animal alone.

I open the car door gingerly – the passenger side, opposite to where Animal is leaning – and get out. I tell Animal I need to pee. He grunts. I walk slowly into the woods, each footfall-crunch amplified, as far as I dare. Then I stop. My heart is thumping so loud I imagine he will hear it. I turn off the torch. I wait a second. I take a few paces. Then I start to run. And I run and I run and the cold night air burns into my lungs, and the adrenalin kicks in and I'm panting and running and running. I get disorientated and worry if I'm running the right way. I have no idea where I am, I am just running through tall forest trees in the middle of the night, and I am breathing so loud and hard, *pwhoo*, *pwhoo*, and the cold air is burning my chest, and I cannot stop. I run on and on. And eventually, after I don't know how long, I reach the road. I reach the road, but I need to keep hidden because it's way after midnight and I'm a nineteen-year-old girl with only a torch, and I certainly don't want to be picked up and go from the fat into the fire.

And then another thought comes into my head: I can't just wait for Ian like we'd arranged. What if the plan has gone horribly wrong? What if, at this very moment, Ian is being attacked? And I am just waiting on the side of the road? I realise I have to get help. I must get the police. So I run along the road, ducking into the forest every time I hear a car. After nearly a mile I see some lights. And thank God it's a motel. I go in and, still panting, slump on the reception desk. I blurt out the whole story. The man at reception looks at me like I'm mad. I make him call the police. He rings the police. I breathlessly tell the police about Animal sleeping against our car and camping in the forest and making notches on my head. The policeman sounds suspicious. They want to know where I am from. I tell them; they are more interested in my nationality than in the situation. I can tell they think I am a crazy woman. The policeman asks me what crime has been committed. I tell them as far as I know no crime has been committed . . . yet. But one could be being committed at any moment. It seems we have got into a semantic discussion about the here and now, what exists, what doesn't exist, what might exist. The policeman tells me they cannot investigate a crime that hasn't been committed. I realise it's useless. Time is hurtling by. Ian could be in mortal danger, or he could be looking for me. I give up with the motel and go back out on the road where I stand by the edge, ready to leap into the forest, looking into the blackness, wondering what the fuck I am going to do next. Waiting. Walking. Running. Not sure where to go. Or where to stop.

And then I see a pair of headlights flaring through the trees and illuminating the bend in the road behind me. I turn. I hear the distinctive puttputtputt of a VW Beetle. Horace! Surely! A VW driving very, very slowly. Kerb-crawling along. Its two white beams coming towards me. And yes! I can make out the white skunk stripe. It *is* Horace. But as I run towards it, my feet suddenly become lead, my stomach plummets to the base of my spine, my skin goes cold. Who is behind the wheel? I approach cautiously. My eyes are fixed on the dark shape of the driver's head. And then I make out Ian's curly hair. But just as he pulls up by my side, again I experience a moment of terror as I realise it might be a trick, that Ian might be driving, but that Animal might be hiding in the back with the knife. Ian opens the door. His face looks white. 'Get in!' he hisses urgently. I look over his shoulder. 'It's all right! Get in!'

We howl with relief. That we are out of it. Away from Animal. Free and alive. Ian says when he told him that I'd gone, that he had frightened me, he stood up, put his sleeping bag over his head and began to sway like a bear. Ian stood there, himself frozen for a moment as Animal swayed. Then he backed slowly towards the car, opened the driver's door, folded back the bed; he said his heart was pounding in his chest, he couldn't look at Animal. He flipped the driving seat around as fast as he could, but his hands were shaking and he couldn't slot it into the runners so he just rested it in position. The keys were in the ignition, thank God. He quickly glanced towards Animal, and amazingly (in my view) said goodbye, then he got into the car, turned on the ignition, and as fast as he possibly could, took off. I am astonished at his bravery, his wherewithal. He even took back the knife!

We drive six miles to the far side of the nearest town then look for a motel. We hide the car round the back. We pay for a room. We put every stick of furniture in the room against the door, but we still don't sleep a wink. The next morning we leave at daybreak.

As we drive through the town of South Lake Tahoe, we see Animal walking down the empty street, sack slung over his shoulder. We both scream. Ian puts his foot on the gas, and I'm too terrified to look back.

THE AMATEUR WAITRESS

I stepped out of the plane onto the passenger stairs, blinking into the early morning southern skies at Auckland Airport, after a forty-eight-hour, five-stop flight with my very new New Zealander husband, Jonathan. It was February 1987, and it was already hot. I had just been sprayed by a man with an aerosol in each hand walking down the plane's aisle wearing shorts and long socks – European bugs (and attitudes) – and I was about to meet my in-laws, waiting for us in Arrivals.

At the bottom of the stairs, three strides across the tarmac, the person in front of me, having heard my English accent, stopped, turned, and asked me what I thought of New Zealand. I looked across the runway towards the terminal building.

'Looks great,' I said.

I had met Jonathan just a few weeks before in the old dog biscuit factory near Tower Bridge on the Thames in London, where he was a breakfast chef in the canteen of the Jacob's Street Film Studios, and where, two floors above, I had been temporarily lent a derelict studio. He had come to the exhibition I'd had in one of the wharf-side warehouses. Each day, after his cooking shift, Jonathan had been collecting all the leftover food, boiling it up in a massive industrial-sized saucepan, and taking it to the South Bank to feed the homeless people who dossed down under the walkways. I offered to drive him in my VW campervan – better, I persuaded him craftily, than the car he'd been lent by the canteen manager. Jonathan had been in England for a year, but his work permit was about to run out. It was just typical of course to meet someone I liked whose work permit was about to run out. And to cut a short story shorter, three weeks later, on Saturday 10 January, for the exhilarating madness of it, we got married in Brixton Registry Office at nine-thirty a.m. Nine-thirty because the price went up after ten a.m., although I distinctly remember I had to fork out twenty-five quid for an emergency licence. The term 'emergency' was what they called any booking within two weeks. 'Emergency?' I joked. 'Desperation more like.' The morning was cold and snow was in the air. Dad drove us to Brixton and turned up the radio full-whack – it was on a local station playing reggae – and we cruised along, deep bass thumping, Dad, in his inimitable way, steering with his knees and clapping the air in those big swallowing cracks I was so familiar with.

And now I was queuing with the aliens, shuffling along foot by foot, clutching my passport, until at last we tumbled out into my new life and the arms of my new family.

We drove through the suburbs, past clapboard wooden

bungalows, unfamiliar trees, red bottle-brush bushes, Jonathan chatting to his family, me in the back, head skewed, nose glued to the window, orientating myself in this new world. Auckland was a low-rise leafy drawl of painted colonial houses set back behind lush front gardens, with big American-type cars and pick-ups parked along the street, all facing the same direction. I was entranced by the leadlight windows and wrap-around verandas and corrugated roofs, and I was entranced by the gardens, alarmingly called *sections*, overflowing with hibiscus and jacarandas and the great fanning leaves of banana trees, and bushes with huge blossoms I had never seen before. It was one of these, 19 Castle Street in the Auckland suburb of Grey Lynn, that we would be lucky enough to call home in a couple of months' time.

Having found somewhere to live, the next thing we had to do was get jobs. So Jonathan went door-knocking with his cordon-bleu chef skills and the boast of having cooked in one of Sydney's best restaurants, You & Me. At the first knock he landed a job at Le Gourmet with New Zealand's celebrity chef of the time, Warwick Brown. Warwick was the smart, rakish, new-rich, no-messing, can-do, inordinately capable kind, whose swish restaurant was in the old fire station in Ponsonby, a twenty-minute walk up the road from our house. Hooray. It seemed logical, with Jonathan's hours, and because we were broke, that I should also get a job in a restaurant. So it was decided. I would waitress.

New Zealand in 1987 was in the giddy bubble of the property and banking boom. Interest rates were 22 per cent, and there were a lot of people who seemed to have *loadsofmoney* and were flashing it about, so the restaurants were noisy, full and very busy. Le Gourmet, being a high-class establishment, only hired experienced waitresses, but further down Ponsonby Road were lots of other restaurants, because Ponsonby Road was *the* restaurant street. There were old, traditional restaurants like Noblio's, with linen tablecloths and carnations in vases, which had been there ever since Jonathan could remember; new, trendy white-leather-and-chrome restaurants; BYO (Bring Your Own – alcohol) restaurants; Italian and Greek and Creole restaurants; and lunch bars – and so off I went, door-knocking.

The Carpet Bagger: no. SPQR: no, sorry mate. Stuff & Waffle: not hiring. Rigoletto's: did I have any experience? Well, no, but what could there possibly be to it? Take the order, bring the food? I worked my way down one side of the street, increasingly despondent as each restaurant turned me away, until I got to the bottom and stood outside Dr Livingstone, I Presume.

I knocked without hope on a thickly painted green door and was just about to leave when a greasy-long-haired, unshaven man with puffy-ringed eyes and flapping socks opened it. The struggle of *not* saying, 'Dr Livingstone, I presume', left me speechless; he certainly looked the part, as if he'd been dragged backwards all the way from Victoria Falls.

'G'day,' he said, without moving his mouth.

'I was just wondering,' I began, cowed and apologetic and very

English-sounding – annoying even to myself, 'if you might be looking for any waitresses?' As if I had a few.

He looked me up and down. My feet got ready to walk away. 'Experience?' he asked bluntly.

'A bit,' I lied.

And I was hired. There and then on the doorstep. I stood there looking dazed. 'Um . . .' What now? I wondered.

'Be here by five.'

'Today?'

'You want a job next year?'

'No, of course, fine, right, yes, thanks, okay, sure,' I burbled. 'Great, see you at five. Bye, then.'

And off I skipped home with my news, the stupid 'Bye, then' reverberating in my ears.

Dressed in what Jonathan advised was waitressing attire – black skirt (which I owned) and white shirt (which I had to buy) – I arrived ten minutes early. I knocked. Nothing. I knocked louder. Nothing. I stood there. I knocked really loudly and the door flew open. Dr Livingstone was still in his socks, eight inches of woollen tongue flapping from the end of his toes, but now he had an apron on, and on his apron was a map – in blood, guts, tomato juice and an awful lot of green.

'G'day,' he ventriloquised, eyes fogged over.

'We met earlier . . .' I foolishly began.

His head, almost imperceptibly, beckoned me in.

I crossed Dr Livingstone's threshold into a jungle world. Murals of waterfalls splashed down the walls, tigers peered from behind rubber plants, rope lianas trailed around door frames, toy parrots perched on branches: Dr Livingstone, I Presume was a *themed* restaurant; even the tables were green.

My first job was to lay the green tables with green leafy just-wipe vinyl-coated tablecloths, and adorn each place setting with a monkey-printed paper napkin. Meanwhile Dr Livingstone stirred a massive stockpot of bubbling broth in the tiny kitchen at the back with the tiny window looking out onto a tiny yard full of overflowing dustbins. Steam billowed out, condensation ran down the tiny window. It was jungle-hot in there. Drops of sweat bubble-wrapped his brow. Where were his sous chefs? I wondered.

This chef, it turned out, did everything himself. Stirred, chopped, prepped, diced, rolled, dunked, butchered − starters, mains, puddings, the lot.

'Um . . .' I stood in the doorway.

Dr Livingstone looked up and glared.

I brought my hands up, open-palmed, into a what-shall-I-do-now? mime.

'Well, *familiarise* yourself with the menu,' he snarled sarcastically.

Dr Livingstone's menus were eighteen inches tall, laminated (no changes, then) and decorated with a drawing of Dr Livingstone in a pith helmet peering out between two giant leaves. Each dish had a jungle-themed name. Cocktails: Jungle Juice, Python Poison and Crocodile Tears. *You know you want to!* the menu exclaimed. The cocktail ingredients − variations of vodka, ginger, pink lemonade, pineapple, lime, Hawaiian punch, strawberries and white rum − were in brackets with a 'witty' quip. Starters: Tiger Tail

Soup (*spicy fish with a bite to it!*), Snake Sizzlers (*spicy bacon croquettes, hiss hiss!*), or Dead Men's Fingers (*salami and avocado – nice and sticky!*). For mains you could have Jungle Stew (*spicy lamb, still jumpin'!*), Jungle Curry (*spicy chicken, still crowin'!*), Cannibal Cutlets (*spicy pork, still snortin'!*), Monkey Mayhem (*spicy beef, still leapin'!*), Piranha Pie (*spicy fish, watch out for your fingers!*) or a Tarzan Burger (*spicy-spicy! Very dicey!*). I smiled, nodded and chuckled as best I could. For dessert there was Dr Livingstone's Jungle Ice (*pineapple ice cream*), Dr Livingstone's Cannibal Ice (*chocolate ice cream and raspberry sauce* – sorry, but that's what it was), or Dr Livingstone's Snake Ice (*kiwi fruit ice cream*).

The list was pleasingly short for such a physically large menu, and I also noticed that everything was incredibly cheap: $4 or $5 for starters, while the mains were only $6 to $10 each.

I checked my watch. An hour before service.

'Um,' I hesitated. 'When are the other waiters coming?' I asked.

Livingstone's lip sweetly curled. 'Yer on yer own, mate.'

He turned back to his jungle stock and threw a kilo of carrots onto his chopping block.

I stared at the two dark circles radiating outwards from his armpits on his blue T-shirt, another growing oval stuck to his back. 'Oh, right,' I said.

I didn't know what to call him, and by now I was too intim-idated to ask. 'Um. Do we have any bookings?' I asked.

'Fifty-four,' he grunted.

'Fifty-four!'

Livingstone was hunched over the chopping board, knife flashing as the diced-carrot mountain grew. Then onions. Then tomatoes. A hill of chopped-up beef. A hill of glistening pinky-white raw chicken. Rivulets of watery blood twisted around islands of pips and peelings, then dripped off the worktop as Livingstone's flapping socks mopped up the floor. Also on the bench were three open boxes of fish fingers.

He turned his testy eye on me. His neck had developed a liver-coloured heat rash with a nasty boil gathering at the end of it like a full stop.

'Right,' I said, my face set in a rictus. 'What about the wine?'

'They bring their own,' he quipped dryly.

'And what, what if, what if they forget?'

'They don't.'

'Oh. Right. Great. Is there a book with the bookings?' I asked.

'Nap.'

I thought he said nap, but I wasn't going to ask. Bloody hell, baptism by fire. Livingstone was still chopping. The kitchen was unbearably hot and airless. Sweat tributaries fanned into a delta down the back of his neck, one hand chopping, the other sweeping food aside. More carrots, a dozen avocados, chop, chop, onions, chop, pineapple rings, chop, sticky syrup everywhere, chop, chop, peppers, chop, chop, pips, stalks, little mounds and hills around the bench, monkey meat slumped in crimson pools, jars of chilli paste and mustard, tomato ketchup bottles with their tops off, a tower of burgers. A new hill, orange and white, the fish fingers, chop-chopped. The Jungle Stew was raging. Indeterminable shapes bobbing in the steam.

'Ow!' Livingstone yelled as he whipped his finger away from

the chopping board and straight into his mouth. 'Plaster!' he shouted, pointing to a cake tin on a shelf.

Now, one thing I did know about kitchens was that chefs used blue plasters when they cut themselves, because only the day before Jonathan had come home with a blue plaster on his thumb. Why blue? I asked. So you can find them easily if they fall off. I rummaged around in the tin but could only find beigy-pink plasters.

Livingstone was sucking his finger, looking at me. Oh, no, I was going to have to put it on his finger! He was sucking hard, then his finger was in front of my nose. Crimson blood began filling a deep-sliced crevice. Trying not to wince, I peeled away the backing and pressed the plaster over the wound.

'Ha!' I shouted weirdly. His hand was hot, wet, and slimy. The blood immediately began to seep through. I looked at the clock. We would be open in ten minutes. There was a rapping at the door. I charged out. Already waiting in the street was a young couple holding a bottle of champagne.

'We're a little early,' the girl said, 'but if you could put this in the fridge for us, we'll come back in five minutes.'

'Bollinger,' I said, reading the label. They smiled. I cradled the bottle of champagne.

'Um. Where's the fridge?' I asked through the billowing steam.

'Out the back.' Livingstone threw his eyes in the direction of the back door. Which wasn't a back door but a door to a long narrow storeroom. You could only just get to the fridge, and when you got there, only just open the door. The freezer compartment was full of snowy ice cubes embedded with peas and crumbs.

22

On either side of the fridge were plastic stacking trays of wrin-
kled courgettes, deflated peppers and sprouting spuds. On the
shelves above were commercial-sized boxes of tomato paste, chilli
spice, BBQ sauce and mayonnaise. At the end of the narrow room
was a camp bed, with a rucked-up blanket and pillow, and just
beyond that was a cat tray full of little cat shits studded with cat
litter, like melting chocolate fingers. I wrestled the champagne
bottle horizontally in beside a bowl of chicken drumsticks, then
blew out a long loud sigh; it was time to open up.

On the counter in the dining room, next to the menus, I
found a note pad and a pen.

Six people came in, laughing loudly.

I smiled broadly: 'Table for . . . six?'

I showed them one table, and they chose another. Two more
people were standing waiting to be seated. Then another six. Then
another couple, and then *another* couple. I started to get in a flap,
back and forth, trying not to show it. And then four more people
walked in. I grabbed the menus. The large table loaded me up
with white wine for the fridge. One table wanted a jug of water.
Did we have beer? No, it was bring-your-own, I told them. They
sniggered. They repeated *bring-your-own* in what I suspected was
meant to be an English accent. Then one of them said, 'It's BYO,'
so one of the guys got up to go and buy some beer. The second
couple were trying to catch my eye, waving their bottle of red.
I rummaged around and found, thank God, a corkscrew among
the cutlery. I opened the wine and put it on the table, as two
more bottles were passed to me. I could feel my face rigidly
sporting a slightly mad smile. Four reds were lined up, and of

course I couldn't remember which table had given me which wine. Three more people were standing at the door waiting to be seated. Bloody hell. A woman at the table by the window was holding up her water glass because I had forgotten the water jug.

I disappeared into the kitchen to find Livingstone in a muck sweat, stirring the jungle stew and chopping an onion at the same time. The sweat was rolling down his nose to the temporary reservoir of a large drop, which swung briefly before it elongated with its own weight to disengage from his nose, and fall, splash, into the stew which he was still stirring. His blood-stained plaster was now also stained with Jungle Stew. Did he notice the shadow of repulsion that flashed across my face? I had a feeling he might have.

'There's no space in the fridge,' I said, each hand carrying two bottles of white wine.

'Take something out then!' The caustic sarcasm in Livingstone's voice sounded like we had been unhappily married for years.

I peered into the fridge and pulled out a plastic container of pink liquid. 'What's the pink liquid?' I shouted.

'Yer cocktails,' Livingstone shouted back, as if I should have known. 'The Python Poison's pink!'

There was another one, bright green. I pulled out a Tupperware box containing some curled-up cheese, an opened tin of pine-apple, a punnet of weeping strawberries and a bowl of something that smelt fishy, and shoved the bottles in. I filled up the jug with water and raced back out.

'Could we have some ice?' the girl asked, peering into the jug.

'No.'

They looked at me.

'I mean the ice isn't quite frozen yet,' I lied.

'We came in earlier,' the very young champagne couple were back and waiting by the counter, 'but you've given away our table.'

'Have I?'

'We booked that table,' they said, pointing to the window table. 'I specifically requested it,' the man said.

'I'm sorry, I'm new and the last waitress took the bookings book with her,' I lied. 'We could ask them to move,' I made a pained grimace, 'or you could sit over here?' I pointed and looked at them imploringly.

They smiled. Thank God, they smiled and sat down. They were kind and sweet and happy and young, and it was clear this must have been a special occasion. I gave them a menu, and in through the door came a party of five. There were now thirty-two people in the restaurant and it wasn't yet eight o'clock. Wine bottles filled the counter, the red to be opened, the white to go in the fridge. I was running from table to table in a very uncool way.

'No, we don't have ice buckets, sorry.'

Then bugger-shit, the table of six *all* wanted cocktails.

'Two Python Poisons, three Jungle Juices and a Crocodile Tears,' I announced to Livingstone, who had a dozen plates lined up on his work bench. You had to give it to him, he didn't hang around.

'Ye-ah?' he said, with challenging mockery.

'I'm sorry, I don't know what to do.'

He threw down his knife, wiped his hands down his apron, and led the way to the fridge.

'Glasses.' He pointed to a tray of funnel cocktail glasses on the bench behind the withered courgettes. On the same tray were a saucer of salt, a saucer of water, a bowl of sliced oranges and a cup of mint sprigs. He turned a glass upside down with the rim in the water, then into the salt, then just sloshed the pink Python Poison from the plastic container straight into the glass, no shaking or anything. He opened the freezer, plunged his hot hand in, wrestled a bit, then brought out a fistful of stuck-together ice and chucked it in the glass with a slice of orange and a sprig of mint.

'Got that?'

'Yup, right, fine.'

'Two Python Poisons, two Jungle Juices and two Crocodile Tears,' I announced proudly as I put them down.

'It was *three* Jungle Juices, *one* Crocodile Tears,' the table of six informed me.

'Oh, sorry,' I retrieved one of the Crocodile Tears and headed back into the kitchen.

As I passed the young couple they looked up and mouthed *champagne*.

I knew how to open a bottle of champagne because Jonathan had shown me. You don't twist the cork, you ease it out slowly with your thumbs, little by little. Nevertheless, I opted to do it in the storeroom to be safe.

POP!

The bloody thing ejaculated, a quarter of the bottle fizzing all over the place. I stared at it and lifted the bottle to the light to see exactly how much I'd lost. A significant amount. And then I went into that cool, calm state I seem to find when things have FUCKED UP BIG TIME and I need to think of something fast.

And what I thought of was to top it up with tap water. I mean, they were young and happy and I really didn't want to spoil their night by telling them their expensive once-in-a-blue-moon treat was all over the filthy storeroom floor. My guess was that they were not champagne connoisseurs. And what would be worse, to get myself into trouble and piss Livingstone off, or . . . top it up? Top it up, I reckoned. They would never know.

I ran the tap for a minute until the water was nice and cold.

'Sorry about the wait,' I said. 'I was just drying the glasses.'

I began to pour a clear pale primrose liquid – with bubbles, thankfully. It looked okay to me. 'Cheers,' I said.

By the time they raised their glasses, I was taking the order from a table of six. I glanced back reluctantly, furtively, poised for them to say something, but no, they were sipping away, oblivious. *Right decision.*

While the young couple were happy and ogling away at each other, the table of four were not. I hadn't taken their order yet, and they were giving me impatient stares.

'Two Tiger Tail Soups, three Snake Sizzlers, one Dead Men's Fingers; two Jungle Stews, a Jungle Curry, one Monkey Mayhem and two Tarzan Burgers,' I repeated back to them.

I went round each table, then back to the kitchen with *all* the orders, which, one by one, I read out then stabbed onto the six-inch nail Livingstone had whacked into the shelf above his workbench.

It was miraculous. Two soups, ladled straight out of the stockpot, a squirt from the fish sauce bottle, a dollop of ketchup, done. Ping, the microwave light flashed, four unfrozen croquettes two by two onto the plates, sprinkled with crispy bacon and a drizzling of Jungle Stew. Dead Men's Fingers, avocado mushed up with salami bits, were squirted out of an icing bag with a giant nozzle, five green sausages on each plate, each with a red fingernail – half a radish – done. I carried them out, not two and one, as an experienced waitress would, but one plate in each hand. I had to ask who ordered what. Some of the orders were mixed up, so some plates had to go to different tables. One woman began to huff and puff a lot. The table by the window wanted their next bottle of wine – no, not that bottle. The young couple wanted a champagne bucket. Annoying. A refill of water, a clean glass, I ran back and forth. Meanwhile in the sweat-zone, Livingstone was ladling the same jungle juice over every dish: a plate of chopped-up fish fingers; a plate of mince; a plate of chicken. As Livingstone prodded a burger in the frying pan with his finger, the wet plaster was flapping like a small flag. The stew raged on, boiling its flotsam, gushing out steam. More ketchup, more Tabasco. Sweat rolling down his face, drip by drip, Livingstone bent over his cauldron and stirred.

Tiger Tail Soup, done; Jungle Curry, done; Monkey Mayhem, done. I flew to the dining room and back to the kitchen, two plates at a time. But I was distracted. For the plaster on Livingstone's finger, the gruesome bloody banner, was barely attached, with now just a corner battling physics and gravity.

Two burgers out of the frying pan into the buns, tomatoes, a dollop of sauce, done.

What could you expect for eight bucks, after all? Livingstone padded back and forth from bench to stove, his socks decorated in onion skin and chilli pips, a bit of chicken skin stuck on the heel. He picked up the wooden spoon, and the next time I looked across the plaster had gone.

Each plate I carried out I scanned for the plaster, but everything was murky green. I tore back and forth – wrong bottle of white wine, *sorry*; wrong Monkey Mayhem, *sorry*; *sorry*, more water, more forced smiles, more *sorries* – eyes sweeping each plate in search of a Jungle Stew-coloured plaster. The tenuous hold I had on the situation was slipping further and further. Mad little squawks jumped out of my throat each time the door flew shut behind me from dining room to kitchen. One table was missing their mains, one was missing two starters, one man said his chicken tasted of fish, another said his Dead Men's Fingers tasted of pineapple (surely a good thing?). And I couldn't find Table Three's bottle of wine, though I was sure they had already drunk it and were being opportunistic. Everyone seemed to be getting a little fed up. Except for the young champagne couple, who smiled every time I went past.

The desserts were the bellows on the hell fire. The kitchen was now so hot that the ice cream melted within seconds of getting it on to the plate, and the plating-up with jungle garnish – sliced strawberry and mint; tinned pineapple and mint; grated chocolate and raspberry sauce – was my job, as Dr Livingstone was sitting outside in the trash-can yard having a fag.

I don't know how I got through it. Livingstone totted up the dockets on his wet worktop, which was still covered in flakes of fish fingers, bits of burgers, chicken skin and drips of Jungle Stew. I ran back and forth with bills and change. Each bill had some kind of discrepancy, the items were wrong, the total was wrong.

Sorry, sorry. When I finally left, at eleven p.m., Livingstone, barely visible amongst the detritus and the Leaning-Towers-of-Pisa crockery, was halfway through a plastic container of Python Poison. Five cigarette butts floated in a pool of melted ice cream. I had three dollars in tips (the champagne couple). Livingstone said he'd call when he needed me again. I knew I wouldn't be hearing from him. Not just because he didn't ask for my number. I knew, as he quartered me with a sullen eye, that I would never get paid. Dispensable one-night waitresses like me were another way to keep his prices down – that and his chameleon stew, which could become any dish Livingstone wanted it to be.

I walked quickly up Ponsonby Road. I couldn't wait to get to the old fire station. I had arranged to meet Jonathan at Le Gourmet after work.

When I arrived the chefs were sitting at a table in the restaurant having a beer. 'How was it?' Jonathan asked as I sat down to join them.

I regaled them with every gruesome detail, the bubbling stew, the storeroom bed, Livingstone's sweat dripping into the stew, the disappearing plaster, the menu of Monkey Mayhems and Tarzan Burgers, the chopped-up fish fingers. Hearing the squeals of horror and roars of delight, celeb chef Warwick Brown pulled up a chair. I finished off with my mishap with the champagne and topping up the Bollinger.

'You *what?*' Warwick's eyes popped out of his head with unconcealed glee. 'Bloody Moses!'

★

The next day I began door-knocking on the other side of the street. At least now I could say I had experience. Within four knocks I landed a job in an Italian restaurant, which lasted long enough for them to realise I couldn't carry three plates down one arm like the other waiters. Then I got a job at the China Rose. That lasted a day: not fast enough. Then I got a job at a Creole restaurant called Mumbo Jumbo. There were other waitresses and a maître d' called Suzanne, whose hair was piled up on top of her head in ringlets. Her hands were so perfectly manicured they made me self-conscious of my own, which I kept behind my back because there was black ink ingrained down the side of my index finger and dark quarter-moons of garden under my fingernails.

I arrived for work at Mumbo Jumbo as smart as I could manage, my white shirt washed, my black skirt ironed, hands scrubbed, and reported for duty. Suzanne looked me up and down and sighed.

'Please go and wash your hands,' she said in an exhausted tone. I went and washed them.

When I came out of the loo she was waiting outside. She clicked her fingers and pointed at my hands. I held them out to her. I told her the ink wouldn't come off.

'Well scrub till it does,' she said. 'We can't have you serving table like that.'

I scrubbed and scrubbed and scrubbed. I showed her my hands. She *tsssked* and walked off. It wasn't going well, I realised. I busied myself helping the other waitresses lay the tables. Everything I did they corrected: moved a knife over, folded the napkin differently. I soon realised the culture of this restaurant came down through the maître d'. I tried to look busy and useful, but was failing at that too. Suzanne, like Livingstone, suggested I familiarise myself with the menu, which unlike Livingstone's was on plain white paper and changed every day. This higher-class restaurant was fusion Creole nouvelle cuisine, which meant the portions were very small but very pretty. It was all the rage. I was put in the section right at the back.

The only pleasure I could look forward to was the moment I could charge up the street and join Jonathan and the chefs at Le Gourmet, who had begun to look forward to the next installment of woe and ineptitude.

Day three at Mumbo Jumbo (I had lasted this long) and it was clear Suzanne would have liked to grind me to a pulp with her sharp heels. Everything I did was wrong. The worse it got, the worse I got. Each time she looked over towards me (which she did frequently) my hands began to shake and the soup spilled over onto the soup-plate rim, and I would have to return to the kitchen to wipe it clean – by which time, as Suzanne testily pointed out, the soup was too cold to serve. This was their busiest time of the week, Sunday lunch, and there were people waiting to be seated. In my section Suzanne sat a family of four, Mum, Dad and their two daughters, dressed in their Sunday best. I could tell immediately from the dad's sunburnt neck, brown as his leather belt, and his massive hands that he was a farmer, and that this was a big day out. They pulled up their chairs, upright, proud and a little uncomfortable. The mum was freshly out of the hairdresser's, her tight curls smelling of hairspray, her floral dress pressed, her pale-blue patent handbag perching like a poodle on her lap. The two daughters also looked like they had just come out of the hair-dresser's, their big blonde roller-curls framing each pretty face. I smiled.

'G'day,' Dad said.

'Special occasion?' I smiled.

They all smiled. It was the youngest daughter's eighteenth birthday.

'Well, congratulations!' I said. 'Happy birthday! Can I get you some drinks?'

Suzanne walked past, her head cocked for her ear to get closer. I handed out the menus. The dad ordered four Cokes with ice and said they *might* order a glass of wine later.

'Ready to order?' I asked about ten minutes later when I saw a lull.

The mother ordered, the daughters ordered, then the father ordered. I looked at the father, knowing what he had just ordered for his main was the equivalent of two radishes, a sliver of fish and four dots of relish in a delightful arrangement.

'If you're hungry,' I ventured, 'I don't think that will be enough. I think you should go for the fish gumbo, which is a kind of thick stew,' I explained. The fish gumbo was the best thing on the menu and, being a gumbo, it was the least nouvelle-cuisine-y looking dish, with the most actual food in it, even including bits of sausage. He smiled gratefully and went with the fish gumbo. Suzanne whisked past, and then the mother and daughters changed their minds and went for the fish gumbo too.

'What on earth are you doing?' Suzanne was waiting for me in the kitchen.

'What do you mean?'

'What on *earth* are you *doing*?' she repeated even more severely, without explaining what she did mean.

'I'm taking orders,' I said.

'I did not hear you *taking* orders,' Suzanne said, almost quivering with rage, 'I heard you *giving* orders. I heard you telling them what they should choose. As if they couldn't decide for themselves. How dare you?' And then she said, 'I can't possibly let you speak to customers. You'd better go and wash up.'

So that was my last day at Mumbo Jumbo. I was running out of road.

Yet two days later I got a job at a restaurant called Starlight. The walls were lavender grey with thin silver stripes, and hung with black-and-white photographs of film stars like James Dean and Marilyn Monroe. On each white tablecloth was a glass vase with a single white tulip. This restaurant was run by a husband-and-wife team: Chris, who was the head chef and ran the kitchen; and Rebecca, who ran the dining floor and was maître d'. I didn't have much experience, I told Rebecca, but I was eager to learn. She showed me where everything lived, the glasses, the cutlery, the corkscrews, and how she liked the tables to be laid. She took me into the kitchen and introduced me to Chris and the other two chefs and the guy who was washing up. There were three other waitresses and a wine waiter, and she told me that we shared the tips equally. This was a completely new experience. Chris went through the menu with me and described each dish. Everything was spotless; the fridge was spotless, the floor was spotless, the cookers were spotless. I would spend the first night just learning and helping the other waiters, Rebecca said.

I concentrated hard. I watched the other waiters carry three or four plates at a time. I helped in the kitchen, and then Rebecca asked me to go to a table of two to get the orders for desserts. That night there were no awful stories for the chefs at Le Gourmet. Things were looking up. It seemed I'd finally got a decent job after all.

Jonathan was also enjoying his job, and so I began working five shifts a week at Starlight, with only the odd slip-up to report. There was a bit of coffee-cup rattling – well, a lot of rattling when I learnt I had a food critic on my table – but although I was slower than the other waitresses, and a bit nervous, and my hands were still a bit inky, and my shoes a bit too practical, and I didn't have the waitress-cool, and often had to ask twice what people had ordered, I was getting tips like the other waitresses, and nobody was getting cross with me, and after work we all sat together round a table with a cold beer.

I had reached my record three weeks when one Friday night Starlight was fully booked, with two shifts on every table. The banker boys were in, and on one of my tables an exceptionally loudmouthed specimen was holding court and being the jock. Raewyn, one of the waitresses, knew him. 'Hi Charlie,' she smiled; he put his right arm round her waist and rested his head on her bosom. Then his arm slid down her back, and as he sent her off he patted her bum. I stiffened. Raewyn laughed and carried on with her tables. Charlie blew a kiss to his girlfriend sitting next to him. (At least I assumed she was his girlfriend, from the fact he had his left thumb slipped down the back of her trousers all this time.) A couple of minutes later Charlie grabbed another waitress and she smiled too.

'Who's the new girl?' he asked, pointing at me. I gave a tight smile and backed into the kitchen to fetch nothing at all.

'So, English girl,' Charlie said, 'you want our order, huh?'

'If you're ready.'

'*If you're ready*,' Charlie mimicked. I smiled feebly.

'*If you're ready. If you're ready*,' he said, looking round at his table. They laughed. I stood there with my pad and pen.

'I can come back later,' I said.

'*I can come back later*,' Charlie mimicked. Everyone laughed again. I stepped back to move away.

'Hey, where you going? We're waiting to order!' Charlie shouted. His table laughed, all eyes on me. I was the amusement.

'What would you like?' I turned to the woman on the opposite side of the table.

Mistake.

'What *I* would *like*,' Charlie interrupted, 'is a decent waitress.'

I smiled, waiting, cheeks burning, with my pad and pen hovering.

Charlie folded his arms, leant back in his chair, and then began to stare me out. 'Well, well. What have we here, a little uptight English girl?' he eventually asked.

'Come here, English girl. Come here.'

I walked round to stand at one side of him, just out of arm's reach. He twisted his chair and gave me a once-over, up and down, like a market cow. My face was burning red. The table laughed. Then Raewyn called me aside and offered to take over the table.

Every time I passed Charlie's table, he made a snooty noise and talked loudly in an English accent. I kept my eyes averted. After service, Rebecca called me into her office.

'Sit down,' she said. I sat down.

'One of our customers has left a very large tip,' she began.

'That's nice,' I said.

'Yes,' she said, 'it is.' And then she made a kind of grimacing face. 'It has a condition attached,' she said. 'That on no account can it be shared with you. Can you explain this? What happened? What did you do?'

'Ah,' I said, heart beating faster.

I told her I didn't think Charlie liked my accent much, and that I hadn't played along with his bum-pinching. I asked her how much the tip was. She said it was $300. Between us that was fifty bucks each, a humungous amount. A fifty-dollar tip was a *big* deal. I felt shit; I felt that this was the first job I'd liked and that it would have been fun to share the big-tip bonanza. I shrugged. But it hurt, and was all the more galling because I thought it was a sly, cowardly way to get back at me. Rebecca said that sometimes customers were difficult, but that she and Chris were trying to launch their business and get a good reputation, and sometimes you just had to take things on the chin and be good-natured. Fine, I said, but he was being really obnoxious. She said she had no doubt he was, a lot of customers were obnoxious, but there were ways of dealing with them.

'Don't worry,' Jonathan said later. 'You were right.'

'It felt shit to be singled out like that. Why did he pick on me?'

I slept badly, and all the next day the injustice kept circling, I couldn't stop chewing it over. It really bugged me. But I still had a job, and the next night I was determined to be a *really* good waitress and that *everything* would go *really* well. Then who should walk in the door but toss-head Charlie with a different girl. The red mist came down. It just came down. Like cutting the cords of a venetian blind.

'So it costs three hundred dollars to pinch bums, does it?' I squared up to him. 'Oh, I see we have a *different* girlfriend tonight. Different one *every* night, is it? How much does that cost? What happened to the other one? How does it feel to be such a big shot? With your show-off tips. As long as you can bully some defenceless waitress who can't answer back. Well, I don't give a shit about your tip,' a statement which my outburst was certainly contradicting, 'just buy everything! Bums. Revenge. Girlfriends. Friends. *Laughs* even. Buy them too.'

A little audience was gathering. Charlie's face was puce and stone at the same time. The new girlfriend's face was puce too. 'Get me the manager!' Charlie exploded.

Rebecca was on the scene in seconds, looking white and serious as she ushered them into her office. I began to gather my things.

I felt strangely unburdened. Then Charlie and his date came out of Rebecca's office, his lip curled sullenly as he walked past, and they left the restaurant.

I sat meekly on the other side of Rebecca's desk. I had been called into her office, and waited silently for the *fait accompli*. Rebecca was busying herself with her papers.

'He wants you sacked,' she said.

I nodded sheepishly.

'I'm not going to sack you,' she said.

'You're not?'

'No, I'm not. I'm not going to be told who to hire in my own restaurant.'

'Really?' I couldn't believe it.

'Really,' she said.

They were nice, Chris and Rebecca, and I did stay working at Starlight for at least three or four more weeks, but it was clear waitressing and I were not well matched. I was very bad at it. I just didn't have the *je ne sais quoi*. I think you need to be a bit sassy to be a good waitress, to care enough but not too much, to have hands that don't shake when you give a restaurant critic his coffee. Not to mention hands that are not covered in ink and fingernails that don't contain half the garden. You need to be able to shrug it off, not seethe at night at bad manners or bad taste. You need to remember where you are and what you are doing, like where your tables are and who's waiting for what, not daydream or get distracted by conversations happening elsewhere, or an idea that might suddenly switch on in your head. And you really shouldn't be too nervous *or* too aggressive with your customers. And so it was that the night of socking-it-back to Charlie marked the beginning of the end of the end-of-service entertainment I was able to serve up to Warwick Brown and his chefs at Le Gourmet.

THE TIDY HOUSE

I had few possessions when I lived in West Cork in the 1980s, but those I had were precious to me. I existed frugally with my Egyptian boyfriend as we worked at odd jobs, painting, gardening, pulling carrots for a pound an hour, and moving from one rented cottage to another. After we parted ways, and I'd met Jonathan in London and got married – and before we left for his New Zealand homeland to meet his family and see his life – I had to pack up my things in Ireland and find somewhere to store them.

It felt sad sorting through my paltry possessions. There seemed something so final about it, so end-of-an-era. Pleased as I was (and thankful) to have bagged such a happy soul, it was a wrench to be leaving Ireland, and every funny day I'd lived there came flooding back.

I had loved it all. The wild winds that charged straight off the Atlantic; the glittering stippled sea beyond High Island and Adam and Eve, to Hare Island and the jutting Stags. I'd lived in houses beside castle ruins, on the edge of cliffs, with seagulls and gannets wheeling and peregrines hunting in the sky. I'd fallen asleep in sheltered gullies pin-cushioned with sea pinks. I had followed the band Toss the Feathers from bar to bar, watched Paddy Keenan fall off his stool playing his uillean pipes in late-night lock-ins at O'Briens, or Casey's or Connolly's, or the Skibbereen Eagle. I had been happy there. Swum the seas. Walked the fields. Foraged the hedgerows. Pulled carrots. Dug potatoes. Sung (my one song) at Connie Burns' Station of the Cross when the priest came to say Mass and bless the house and the poteen came out and everyone got pie-eyed drunk. There was no better life. No better place. In my eyes, it was where I felt I could belong. The moment I landed on Irish shores my shoulders dropped three inches just with the relief of being there. And that was not just because of the twenty-four-hour journey from London's Victoria Bus Station to Skibbereen in a smoke-filled Slattery bus.

And now here I was, in my tiny rented cottage in West Cork, sitting amongst my few books, my cups and plates and saucepans, my clothes and towels and sheets, and a pile of newspaper and three empty tea chests, becoming quite maudlin over it. I had made Jonathan agree that we would come back in a year – maybe he could get a job on one of the commercial fishing boats out of Union Hall.

I gave my writing desk away. I gave away my old sofa with the dropped arm. I gave away the counterpane off my bed. But there were some things I couldn't give away. The miniature china tea set I'd had since I was four. A small Victorian toy seal, made, worryingly, now I contemplated it, from real seal fur. The box of treasures I had amassed from the archaeological excavations of my childhood in the garden of 75 High St, Fareham, where

I grew up – flints, feathers, stones, birds' eggs, a tiny glass perfume bottle, a glass poison bottle with POISON written on it, a meteorite, some gold bugs, four diseased leaves I had picked from a bush for their beauty and which still bore their kaleidoscope of fractal scars, and best of all, a clay pipe with a jester's face moulded onto the front of the bowl, completely intact. I put the pipe to my nose, inhaled its chalky earth smell. And the Beatles cake decoration of the Fab Four with Ringo's drum set and everything, which my mother had put on my eighth birthday cake, which she'd made in the shape of a guitar. There were the shells I found on Berria Beach in Spain, where we used to free-camp for a whole month every year on the dunes like gypsies, and where I had gone missing with my cousin, Tony, and my brother, Patrick, on the mountain by the beach (which probably isn't quite a mountain if I were to see it now), and where we had stayed crouched in the undergrowth all night in case we walked off the cliff and into the sea. And then there was the embroidered Guatemalan *huipile* with the tropical flowers twining around the neckline, which I'd bought in a market near Lake Atitlán from an Indian women with betel-juice-stained teeth. And the woollen jacket with the emerald-green quetzal birds on the back that I wore riding on top of the train in the Andes from Riobamba past the snowcapped volcano of Cotopaxi. I know because there is a photograph of me wearing it, sitting on the corrugated roof at the end of the carriage by the brake, in one of my South American photo albums, which of course I also couldn't throw away. And the Spanish fan a boy gave me in Barcelona, where I worked as an au pair in 1975. These weren't just things. They were my life. The red Indian bead necklace from my first love, my grandfather's tinted postcards of horses, from Kerry, before Dad was born, hundreds of them, which he gave me because I was horse-mad. These were things that fingerprinted moments in time, and transported me back to those moments. So I wrapped them up carefully. Three tea chests, heavy with history. And we nailed on the lids.

It was a strange thing, that in all the space we had in West Cork – in our small community of fishermen and carpenters and painters and writers and poets and drop-outs and gardeners and expat English and Germans and Dutch living in old houses rebuilt from wet ruins purchased for very little – no one seemed to have any room. It was hard to believe. Maybe it was because we were an industrious lot: we stored vegetables and made wine, and smoked fish, and collected things, and rarely threw anything away in case it came in handy. So it was a hard task finding someone willing to store my three tea chests for a whole year. Eventually an English guy called Tim, who was caretaking Sean the electrician's house while he was working in Dublin, agreed to let me put my tea chests in Sean's attic, out of harm's way. Jonathan heaved them up. My life. My fractal leaves. My clay pipe. My Guatemalan *huipile*.

We said our goodbyes, sitting outside the Glandore Inn with pints lined up along the harbour wall. Then we tore ourselves away.

It wasn't a year, but a year and a half before we returned to Ireland. New Zealand and Jonathan's family had been kind to us, we'd worked in different jobs (the good and less good); made friends; run a lunch bar together; we'd surfed and swum in the warm seas; barbequed fish on the beach; camped in the wilds; but I missed Ireland terribly. I missed the landscape, and my friends, and the craic, and oddly even the weather. So when our ferry slowly pulled into Cobh harbour I could have almost leapt off it. Ireland had become the promised land. Where I had put all my future dreams and all our hopes. I was eager to get back to my old haunts, have a drink in the pub, shop at Fuller's in Union Hall, walk old paths, visit friends, find us somewhere to live, and retrieve my precious things.

But for some reason Tim seemed oddly content to leave the tea chests exactly where they were. For the moment. He was not living in Sean's house anymore. He was living in Declan's house just down the road. And he now had a girlfriend, he told me; she was English too, and she had two kids.

'An instant family,' I said. 'That's great, Tim. Where is she?'

'Well, we have sort of split up,' Tim said. 'Temporarily.'

He was sitting in the glass porch of Declan's house smoking roll-ups and chain-drinking cups of tea.

'Getting back to the tea chests . . .' I persevered.

But Tim was too busy to sort it out *right this minute*. They were now at the back of Declan's shed, which was full to the brim.

And this went on. And on. Days slid into weeks. And every time I asked Tim if I could get my tea chests now, there was a hitch. It was never convenient. The shed was too full. The padlock was broken. The key was mislaid. He would fish them out. Soon. But not that day.

'What's the hurry?' he drawled, roll-up stuck to his bottom lip, making me feel all hasty and New World.

I didn't know what to do. I wanted to believe the padlock was broken, and I didn't want to mar the picture I'd painted of my beloved place. But I was suspicious. Something was not quite right.

'Something is not quite right,' I finally admitted to Jonathan.

'What do you mean?'

'He won't get my tea chests out.'

'I'll go round.' This was the New Zealand way.

'No, don't.'

'Then you go round, and tell him you're not leaving until he hands them over.'

I went round and told Tim I was not leaving until I got my tea chests, that I needed them, that waiting two months was long enough. Tim hung his head. He said he suspected things might have got a little damp. That mice might have got in. He fetched the chests.

Carried them from the shed. Very easily. For they were very light chests now. Indeed, their lids had been levered off and splinters of plywood jagged away from the nails, forming rough wooden stars around the square rim. I peered inside. The silver-foil lining glinted and crackled emptily, torn shreds flopped sadly down. A couple of broken mugs floated amongst some old jumpers, photographs and torn books at the bottom, like bobbing potatoes in a stew. There was also a child's sock. And a baby's bottle.

'Tim!'

He hung his head some more.

'Tim?' My mouth was open. My mind was whirling. This was inconceivable to me. 'What happened?'

He went on the attack. 'You went away.'

'I told you I was going away.'

'But you said a year.'

'A year. Yes. But it's only a year and a half.'

'Well, I didn't know you were coming back.'

'You did. I said I was.'

'You left. What do you expect?'

'What do you mean, *expect*? I *expect* to come back and find my tea chests unransacked. I trusted you.'

'Well,' he said.

'What happened?' I asked imploringly, in an alarmingly high register.

'I don't know what happened,' he glared. Then walked off.

I ran after him, now angry. Incensed and wronged! He shut the door on me. Wouldn't come out. I was at a loss as to what to do. And I could not believe it. I just couldn't grasp that someone – I already suspected who – had jemmied off the nailed-on lids of my tea chests. Actually levered them off with a crowbar. I returned to the tampered chests. A rattling of detritus in each. I poked around. Where was my box with the leaves, and the clay pipe with the jester's head on the bowl? I searched frantically but they were not there. Nor was my Guatemalan *huipile*. Nor the embroidered belts. Where were my old *Rupert* annuals? Gone. My drawings, gone. My sketchbook, gone. My jacket with the quetzals, gone. The books were scribbled on, 'The Lament for Arthur O'Leary' poem scrawled over, green crayon and a picture of a house drawn over 'Finistère'. A subterranean heat began to rise. My blood steaming and charging through my body in frothing ferment. Then, a sudden chill in the pit of my stomach. Oh no, oh no! I scrabbled in the boxes in panic. Please no. Kept safe for twenty years. My precious Beatles cake decoration with 'The Beatles' actually written on the drum, with Ringo playing it, and the others with their guitars, inch-high in grey suits. But no, oh woe, not here. Fury. Devastation. Rage. I had been wronged most brazenly. I picked the tea chests up, one by one. Loaded them in the car. Face set, I drove off in a dirt spitting wheel-spin blaze.

'What do you mean, ransacked?' Jonathan said.

'Everything is gone, or ruined. Someone has been through all my stuff!'

'No!'

'Yes!'

'Wanker!'

Jonathan wanted to go round – in the New Zealand way. But I said I had to deal with this myself. I went to see my friend Mary, who was also a friend of Tim's. She told me that last year she had seen Tim's girlfriend, Diane, wearing my skirt. Then, she said, Diane was seen at a wedding wearing my Guatemalan *huipile*.

'What?'

'Yes.'

'No!'

Mary said she assumed I had given my things away.

'Oh no!' I said.

'Oh dear,' said Mary.

I was on the war path. I needed a conversation with this Diane. I knew who she was. I knew where she worked. But when I went looking for her she was not there. The shop where she worked – a second-hand junk shop, coincidentally – was shut. It looked like it was closing down. Then I saw her in Skibbereen – my best friend Helen O'Sullivan pointed her out to me; she was coming down the street towards us. I stopped in front of her. She side-stepped me. I side-stepped her back so she couldn't pass.

'Um, Diane,' I said.

'What?' she said aggressively. West Cork is a small place. She had heard I was after her, she knew I knew about the tea chests and how I felt about it.

'Um, I would like my things back,' I said righteously.

'I haven't got your bloody things,' she said.

Helen had cravenly slipped into the supermarket.

'Well, how come you've been seen wearing them?' I said.

'Sod off,' she said. And walked on.

I trotted after her like a mad woman repeating myself: 'I want my things, I want my things.'

She swerved into the car park, got into her car and slammed the door. People were looking at me. My face was all red. Sweat beading on my brow. She gave me two fingers and drove away.

I got nowhere in the quest to retrieve my things. Nowhere with Tim, who told me he was not getting back together with Diane after all, so it was nothing to do with him. I told him it was his responsibility. My things were in his charge. He must retrieve them. He disagreed.

At night it ate away at me. I couldn't let it drop. I went over and over it. I went on and on, bored everyone to death. Everyone was sick of hearing how I lost my things, how my past was stolen by that harpy witch. Jonathan said I should try and let it go. How could I let it go? What about my Beatles cake decoration? And my fractal leaves? And the shells of my childhood? And my grandfather's horse postcards? Why would anyone want them, except me? It was a heinous crime. No one should be able to just get away with something like that. I obsessed, and I obsessed. I painted a big oil painting of an empty box with a baby's bottle in the bottom, with strange Pandora birdlike creatures flying out wearing Guatemalan *huipiles* and smoking clay pipes. I put it in a group exhibition in the Triskel Gallery in Cork. But it didn't have the desired effect, for the transgression was still in my head. I was still cross. Every time I thought of it, I raged.

'Anyway, where does she live, exactly?' I asked Helen one day. They had children at the same school.

Helen told me. 'But I wouldn't go round there, I'd say,' she said. 'That Diane can be a nasty piece of work.'

I decided to get my things back myself. I was going to *take* them back. I resolved to *steal* them back. When Diane was out. It would be easy. Why hadn't I thought of this before? No one locked their doors in West Cork. Ignition keys rusted in ignitions because there was no crime. Except for hippies, of course, smoking their *marra-jewarna*. But still, *marra-jewarna* or no *marra-jewarna*, these were the days when you left your door open, because nothing was ever stolen. Except the precious things from my boxes in the trusted care of my friend. So, I would just walk in when Diane was not there and take my stuff back, I thought. And she wouldn't be able to do a thing about it. I smiled when I thought of her face. The realisation. Ha! The cold clunk of her heart, the soaring of mine. Justice.

I drove to a small horseshoe close of new houses at the back of the village of Rosscarbery, just as Helen described. It was eleven a.m. On the seat beside me sat a large hessian bag with two strong handles for my swag. I parked outside. Sat for a moment checking up and down the street. I knew she was out, but I knocked all the same. No answer. I tried the door, surreptitiously, *hum-di-dum-di-dum*, the handle didn't turn. It was locked! I tried again. I pushed. I nodded to myself, only a thief would lock their house in West Cork. I went round the back. I tried the door. Ah, the handle turned. I called out, as if I knew her. *Diane, hello?* My best friend. *Diane?* Nothing. My own heart thumping. I opened the door. I was in.

I moved quickly. Kitchen. Sitting room. Upstairs. Bedroom. I couldn't find anything. I went to the wardrobe. Dresses, but not my dresses. No *huipile*, no woollen quetzal jacket. I was starting to sweat. I wanted to be in and out, not poking around like this. I was expecting to find my things easily. But none of my books were in the bookcase, nothing was here. And I was perplexed. Because it was, well, so much tidier than I had expected. So clean and neat and ordered, and not what I had imagined at all. The kitchen sink was not full of dirty dishes, nor were there any sick-looking geranium plants, or ashtrays, or marrows hanging in slings. And the drawers were so neat and tidy when I slid them open on smooth runners. And everything was ironed. And I wasn't expecting to have to open any drawers in the first place. But there was no trace. She couldn't possibly have been expecting me. I picked up a photograph on the mantelpiece to see if she was wearing my skirt. But it was not Diane in the photograph. I picked up the next photograph. I didn't recognise anyone at all. Not in this family group of husband, wife and three children. And that was the moment I realised I was in the wrong house.

Which of course was exactly the same time that I realised I was *burglarising* the wrong house. Which was followed a few seconds later by the realisation that I was a burglar. And that any minute someone might come home. And while these realisations were stampeding through my brain, there was, simultaneously and paradoxically, a horrible *stuck* moment. As if it all dawned in a collision. Or needed time to compute. In a nauseous wave. Like a cartoon moment, a butter-side-down bread moment, a ghastly sick feeling hovered above me in the Irish air, a swaying on the spot and a cold sinking when all my blood slumped into my feet and I couldn't move. When I saw the headlines of the *Cork Examiner*. And the *Southern Star*. Then the glue unstuck, I pirouetted round on the ball of one foot, and as fast as a rabbit I was back down the stairs and standing at the front door. In my panic my hand couldn't find the button on the door latch. My heart, mind, soul, spirit, desire, were already in the car, but my body was still standing on the wrong side of the door. *Come on, come on.* I went to the back door. I was out! I walked fast and in a ridiculous fashion down the side of the house, then round the front, and across to the car. Again the handle-function eluded me. I have heard how people in air disasters and car crashes can die because in their panic they can't open their seat belts. Something like that was happening to me. Then the car door opened and I was in the car. I turned the key – thank God I'd left it in the ignition – and the beautiful noise of the engine roared into life as I drove jerkily away. Down the close, left, right, out onto the Skibbereen road, and then an involuntary jerk as my shaking right foot flipped off the accelerator, the car lurched, and my shoulders slumped forward. Oh!

And my mouth probably gaped open, for I'd left my great big swag bag in the middle of the living-room floor.

THE EXCITING INVITATION

In 1990 Jonathan and I were back in Auckland. We had been living in Ireland for a year and a half in a very damp and tiny two-room cottage at the end of a pier called, appropriately enough, Pier Cottage. From our bed, early in the morning with the door open, we could watch an otter on his back in the bay, so close we could hear him crunching through his breakfast. Jonathan crewed on a commercial fishing boat, and I painted in the second room. But now it was Jonathan's turn to be homesick. He missed his family and his parents were getting on – and they missed him. The distances between our homelands couldn't be further and each upheaval was daunting, and expensive, and painful. This would become the pattern and dilemma of our life together. Where we would be. What we would do.

This time, not tempted to return to our former restaurant lives – terrible hours, bugger-all money – we had enrolled as mature students to study at Auckland University. We were hoping to find our feet in New Zealand, and make up for our very different but similarly gappy educations. I was studying Fine Art at the

Elam School of Fine Arts; Jonathan was studying Politics in the main university. We had both dropped out of the normal course of our 'expected' lives. He had been a primary school teacher, then a cordon-bleu chef in a smart restaurant in Sydney, and had then decided to walk across Spain; I had been upping sticks from different places and different situations trying to make a go of something . . . and now we were here. We had married on a wild whim after three weeks, but then I'd always had a nose for a wager. We had flown back and forth across the world together and were trying to make a life. For me in New Zealand everything *was* new. New family, new weather, new landscapes and seas, new critters such as possums and wetas, new birds like wax-eyes and tuis and fantails, and even fruit that I'd never tasted before. Oh feijoas! There was even a completely different night sky. There is something liberating about starting afresh. But here the possibilities for reinvention, in a place where one had no past, seemed boundless. And for the first time in my life I was doing all right in an institution. I was ten years older than the other students, and about ten years younger than most of the lecturers, so straddled a sort of in-between gap, but being an older student meant that you tended to *listen*, and I quickly discovered it was all very interesting, and the teachers were exceedingly good, and everything felt contemporary and pulsating with a kind of energy I had not experienced at school, and new worlds began to open up to me.

Every chance I got I would enrol to study an English course in the main university to credit towards my Fine Arts degree. One of these courses was American Language Poetry taught by Michele Leggott and Roger Horrocks, who between them bombarded us each week with mind-bending contemporary American poetry by poets like Robert Creeley and Lyn Hejinian and Charles Olson and Susan Howe and Lawrence Ferlinghetti and Adrienne Rich. Afterwards, for coursework, we had to respond to these lectures in our workbooks by discovering links and connections, and we were encouraged to express our own thoughts and ideas, so that our learning spiralled outwards. This was new to me, and suited me very well; and I flourished. And miraculously our tutors read every word in every one of their students' workbooks, and interacted and wrote comments down the side. I felt liberated, which was in turn reflected in my work at the art school, where I was lucky enough to have a lecturer in printmaking called Carole Shepheard, who was not only an excellent teacher, but an artist who generously shared all her own methods and discoveries. With every printmaking technique she taught us – lithography, etching, screen-printing, woodcuts and linocuts – we tried to push each method as far as we possibly could. And all the gear to do it with was at our disposal. The combination of all this – the American poetry, the printmaking, the art theory and the fashion at the time of raiding high and low culture – sent me into a creative frenzy. With each new work I wanted something Bigger, Better, Different! There was a lot of strutting one's stuff at art school, but it was also a communal bonanza of experimentation and young excitement where everything seemed fresh and new. The culmination of all this for me was deciding to do an enormous composite print in six pieces, using every printmaking technique there was, in which I was going to tell the story of, well, er, basically, Life.

I had already begun to veer off towards storytelling in my work, indeed I was writing all over my paintings and prints – including scientific data about the life cycle of the albatross, or an iceberg, or lab mice, or literary observations about some Beckett character or a great Irish chieftain, mixed up with astronomy or biology or newspaper headlines. But this print, I decided, would be the most technically ambitious so far. And I would call it *Who are we? Where do we come from? Where are we going?* referencing Gauguin's famous painting (art reference: tick), not just for the prerequisite post-modern nod, but because I *had* fretted over The Meaning of Life for years. Not that I couldn't see the irony; I was happy to mock the impulse and futile ambition. I set to, with the lithograph stones and the etching acid and the chemicals of the screen-printer's trade, in and out of the darkroom, I scratched and gouged away at wood and lino with sharp instruments, and dissolved ink with fierce thinning agents that almost knocked you out, I transferred newspaper headlines, and carved into potatoes, and collected and borrowed and stole until I was quite pleased with myself.

A floating mono-printed head looked out across a surreal landscape where dark clouds hovered over a caravanserai of linocut camels loping eastward towards a dangerous hazard: a lake of woodcut crocodiles. Above them, delicately etched corn-on-the-cobs zoomed like rockets amongst a hail of Stone-Age arrows. Three dark volcanoes blew their tops beneath Brâncuşi's *Endless Column*; Joseph Beuys' *Fat Chair* (a chair with a triangle of fat on it) perched in the desert alongside ink-thick lithographs of Plato's cave, about to be invaded by an army of ants. And across this mad acreage were printed messages and scraps of 'found' poetry, and copy taken from ads: 'Arrive in Style'; 'Meet Your Competition'; 'The In Group', I transferred 'MASSIVE TROUBLE' next to the crocodiles. And I was pleased as punch. And this big-fish-eat-little-fish arty-myth-parable *thing* went on public display in the end-of-year university exhibition, and a week later I received a message that someone wanted to buy it. I can't remember if it was $200 or $300, but it was a lot for a student who needed the money, and a feather in my cap. The person who wanted to buy it turned out to be a professor in the English Department, Michael Neill. I hadn't taken any of his courses but his reputation went before him: a world-renowned Shakespeare scholar with a trail of authoritative books a mile long, so I was clucking loudly at home at this development. Then I received a telephone call from Michael Neill who said he would like me to frame the print, which he would pay for (a relief, because it was very big and would not be cheap to frame); and would I deliver it to his home and help him hang it in his hall; he said he had just the place.

So I had it framed, and we arranged a day to go and hang it, and we wrapped it in blankets and got it into a van, which Jonathan drove to the address we'd been given, and we rang the doorbell, and Michael Neill opened the door and we said hello and shook hands, then carried the print inside. It was large and unwieldy and heavy, but eventually we manoeuvred it down the stairs, into the hall, and after securing three screws into the wooden-panelled wall, we hung the print and stood back. Michael seemed delighted, and I was particularly delighted that it had found such a good home. And then we met his wife, who quickly disappeared pursuing a couple of small children who ran in and then out. We had a beer, and he asked me if I had read *Wide Sargasso Sea*, which I hadn't (but I remember making sure it was my next book). Michael told us that his brother was a keen art buyer, who he was sure would be interested to see my work, and we nodded, and drank our beer. Then we said goodbye and off we went.

And that was that. Until about six weeks later, the phone rang and Jonathan passed it over with wide eyes, saying, 'It's Michael Neill.'

'Hello, Michael,' I said tentatively, thinking the worst – that the paper had curled or fallen off the mount, or the screws had come out and the frame had fallen off the wall and smashed and the shards of glass had ripped into the print, and that a child had been under it and was now possibly brain-damaged.

But no, Michael was ringing to invite us to dinner – if we were free, he politely added, on a date that was three months hence. Well, the long lead-time kind of threw me: I had never been to any event with so much notice before, except maybe a wedding (certainly not ours), but of course I politely accepted and thanked him and put down the phone.

'We've been invited to dinner,' I told Jonathan in a bemused tone of voice, 'in February!'

Our minds boggled. Not just the time-span, but the very invitation itself. A mere student going to a professor's home for a social engagement? We were frankly amazed, and at the same time I was a bit nervous, for while it was a glimpse into a world I aspired to, I suddenly did not feel at all equipped to hold my own. What on earth was I going to talk about? I certainly couldn't talk about Shakespeare (even though, bizarrely, I'd once learnt *As You Like It* off by heart). I wasn't even sure I could talk about Art – I had appalling visions of regurgitating my last lecture. And who would be there? Maybe his brother, the art collector? We joked about hitting The Big Time.

I could hardly mention this, of course, to any of my fellow art students. Maybe we were all invited, and nobody was mentioning it. But I surreptitiously brought up Michael Neill's name in a discussion about which English courses other students were doing. Was anyone doing Shakespeare? I innocently asked. Nobody was. But a bright rusty-haired sculpture student called Dean asked if I knew who Michael Neill *was*.

'He's the head of the English Department,' I said, 'the professor of Shakespeare.'

'Yes, but do you know who he is?'

'What do you mean?'

'Who his brother is?'

I didn't know.

'Sam,' Dean said.

'Sam?' I said.

'The actor!' Dean said. 'Sam Neill.'

'*The* Sam Neill?' I asked.

'Yes.'

'Really?'

'Yes.'

'Sam Neill of the film, *My Brilliant Career*?'

'Yes!'

'Oh. Right. Blimey.'

And I walked off a bit dazed, because I had loved *My Brilliant Career* when I'd seen it, and I was a bit of a fan of Sam Neill.

'Ha!' Jonathan said. 'The thinking-woman's crumpet.'

'Oh . . . Come on! But, but . . . Wow. Sam Neill!'

And so I began to fantasise . . . Could Sam be the brother Michael was talking about? And could Sam possibly be coming to dinner in three months' time? Which would account, possibly, for the long lead-up. And bloody hell, might I actually *meet* Sam Neill? There followed the extraordinary possibility that in three months' time The Sam Neill might very well cast his eyes upon my huge composite print, of which I was enormously proud, *Who are we? Where do we come from? Where are we going?* We were going to dinner, we joked. On the road to My Brilliant Career, Jonathan teased. And so we fooled about, the jokes madder and more surreal, until the apprehension and excitement were almost too much to bear. But nothing would stop the anticipated dinner growing in our imaginations, for after all there was plenty of time for it to grow, and grow.

In the meantime I looked Sam up. Of course I did. I learnt his age, his list of films and parts, that he had been married and divorced and that he now had a Japanese wife. Which was common enough, I'd noticed, in Australia and New Zealand. Far less common for Japanese husbands to have New Zealander wives I should add. Then a friend told us about a film being made on the west coast of New Zealand at a place called Kerikeri; his brother, who ran a plant nursery, had supplied all the plants. Could this film have any connection with Sam Neill, and the dinner party? Slowly, as the date approached, our imaginations inflated the possibilities of this dinner out of all proportion. That we had ever been invited, considering the guest list we'd drummed up, was a thing of wonder.

The appointed evening finally arrived. The spreadeagled pile of discarded outfits grew mountainous on the bed, but eventually, scrubbed up, dressed up, we set off to Michael Neill's house in our sort-of car, our Skoda. We arrived and parked round the corner just out of view, and walked gingerly up the wooden steps to the front door. And rang the bell. A child opened the door and let us in. We followed the child, and there was Michael, intercepting us. It appeared we were the first to arrive, which was very unlike us, but it was too late to drive round the block now.

'Come in, come in,' said Michael, looking pleased. 'Come down to the kitchen and meet my brother.'

We followed Michael, me chattering about the convoy of Hell's Angels we saw on the way, trying to cover my nervousness as we went into the kitchen. In the corner, standing by the dresser, was a man who looked a bit like Sam Neill. But not quite. No, I definitely didn't recognise him. He had the most enormous whiskery sideburns I'd ever seen, and was quite hairy. In fact, he was *very* hairy.

Michael said, 'Keggie and Jonathan, I want you to meet my brother, Nigel.'

Nigel. Ah. Brother Nigel, of course, the art-collector brother, *Nigel*. I smiled and stretched out my hand, and I said, 'Hello, pleased to meet you, Nigel.' I wanted to burst out laughing, but of course I didn't. We all shook hands. And I was completely wrong-footed, after all our capers and clowning and the tomfoolery build-up, after the fashion parade at home, after the bragging and against-my-better-judgement imagining, I was tongue-tied and hadn't a clue what to say. Then, even more confusingly, a Japanese woman walked in and she was introduced, and we shook hands and said hello to her. Ah, another brother with a Japanese wife. The doorbell went. Nigel smiled and rushed out to answer it. I caught Jonathan's glance and we both raised our eyebrows very slightly at each other and smiled. And slowly the guests arrived. The great and the good, as far as we were concerned. The literati of New Zealand. People we had seen on TV. This writer, that poet, a distinguished Maori actress, the playwright Maurice Shadbolt, the writer Elspeth Sandys . . . Then Jonathan's Politics lecturer arrived: Andrew Sharp, one of the most eminent political scientists in the world, a friend of Michael Ignatieff, with a reputation across Auckland University and beyond for the incomparably brilliant lectures that he delivered breathlessly and fluently without notes. Jonathan was suitably overawed, because Sharp was Jonathan's hero and marked Jonathan's essays. It was kind of unnerving and now we both felt we had snuck in the side door, two imposter students about whom everyone must have surely been wondering '*Who are they? Where do they come from? Why on earth are they here?*'

They all knew each other, and I became shyer and increasingly out of my comfort zone, as Michael was busy telling everyone about my print, which he escorted each guest separately to see. This was undeniably flattering, and so I was at the same time pleased yet deeply embarrassed in such rarefied company, particularly as I still couldn't think of anything to say. So I smiled and drank my wine and ate the tasty snacks that were coming round on trays, which was exactly what, I noticed, Jonathan was doing too. Then we were seated in the dining room. I was placed on the left side of Nigel at the far end of the table, but Nigel had an old friend on the right of him, and they were catching up, so I clung on to the conversation opposite me, but I was also a bit distracted thinking about the weird coincidence of two brothers, Sam and Nigel, looking so similar and also both having Japanese wives. I noticed that Nigel was wearing a very expensive-looking shirt. Which made my charity shop cotton shirt with raffia Pacific Island dancers stitched around the collar look, well, quaint would be generous. And as I sat there, next to Nigel, I couldn't help noticing that he sounded quite a bit like Sam. But then siblings do; on the telephone, my sister Nicky and I are almost indistinguishable. The conversation at my end of the table was about Maori land rights, of which I knew nothing, so I was nodding in a knowing and interested way, even though I was distracted, thinking that soon I would probably be talking to Nigel about his art collection or something else out of my realm, and still feeling extraordinarily shy, because there was something niggling at me, that made me uneasy in a kind of oblique way, because I was not a hundred per cent sure (I certainly wouldn't have bet my life on it) that I was *not* sitting next to Sam. And one reason I was confused about this was that the other guests, who all appeared to know Nigel, said things to him that suggested he was an actor too, things about directors, and producers, and wardrobes and make-up artists, and writers and screenplays, and books that had been made into films.

This uncertainty was deeply unsettling and enough to put me in a quandary (as if I wasn't already) as to what on earth to say when I did speak to him. I could hardly ask him what he did!

But of course this was Nigel, who had been introduced, and collected Art. All our stupid pre-dinner, meeting-Sam build-up had obviously got so deeply into my brain it was reluctant to let it go. For how utterly weird, I was thinking, how ironic it would be to sit next to a Hollywood film star for a *whole* evening without knowing it – a film star whom you were a fan of, like Sam Neill – and not be sure if you were sitting next to him or not. To spend the evening wondering if it were him. With no one to ask. How surreal that would be. And if it *were* him, even more surreal. To be having the experience, but not to know you were having it.

Then Nigel turned to me and asked if I had ever been to Northern Ireland. I had to say I hadn't, that I had lived in southern Ireland, but never crossed the border. He told me he used to go, but hardly went there now. And I asked him about his art collection. And we played out a string of artists' names, artists whose work he owned, and they were well-known New Zealand artists like Billy Apple and Ralph Hotere, and it was a serious top-league collection. And then I couldn't think of anything else to say. And I noticed Jonathan was getting louder across the table. He was sitting next to Elspeth Sandys, and they were laughing about something – he was not confused about whom he was, or whom he was *not,* sitting next to. It was getting late, and Jonathan had taken it upon himself to charge up people's glasses. Jonathan was in wine wonderland. For the wines were unbelievable. Even I could recognise that we were drinking spectacular stuff. A white burgundy, some amazing pinots, and with pudding, some sticky Sauternes. Jonathan knows a bit about wine and I could see he was impressed, and also that he had sampled quite a lot of it. And Nigel seemed to be very interested in it too, as you could tell by the way he twirled his glass, looking at the colour in a scrutinising, pleasurable way.

'One of yours, Sam?' Jonathan asked.

Sam? I blushed for Jonathan's sake (and mine) and tried to catch his eye to save him saying it again. Nigel politely replied, something about some vineyard whose name I can't remember. Then, swallow me whole, Jonathan did it again: something, blah, blah, *Sam.* I glared at him. What was he doing? But no one seemed to bat an eyelid. Then Elspeth called Nigel *Sam.* They all started calling him Sam. Except Michael. Who, being host, had not been hooking in to the nectar like his guests. So was it Sam? Or was everyone drunk? But it was after midnight, and whether it was Sam or not, the evening was over and we really had to go.

And so we backed out of the house, down the wooden steps and round the corner. I cast an eye over my shoulder as we got into our Skoda. I pulled out from the kerb and turned to Jonathan.

'So. Was that Sam?'

He looked at me, dumbstruck. 'What?'

'You called him Sam.'

'What? You didn't realise? You've got to be kidding!'

I groaned.

If I had researched more diligently I might have learnt that Sam's christened name was Nigel. To have had the experience of sitting next to Sam Neill, yet at the same time not had it. To have, in reality, sat next to him *all night,* yet in my un-reality – my reality of the time – I had sat next to a hairy-faced bloke called Nigel.

And so when Jonathan and I watched *The Piano* the following year, with everyone else in New Zealand, everyone in the cinema pointing out the landmarks – the Kerikeri beach with its black sand and the rolling white waves of the powerful Tasman Sea, and the dense tropical New Zealand bush with its giant tree ferns, and other wonderful plants probably from our friend's brother's nursery – what I was looking at was the art collector, my dinner companion, Nigel Neill, walking down the beach in those hairy mutton-chop sideburns.

Years later, living in England, I met Michael again when he became the visiting Professor of Early Modern Literature at the University of Kent. He had tracked me down and we – Michael, his American wife Kube, Jonathan and me – all had lunch together in our garden in Wiltshire. Michael told me that my print *Who are we? Where do we come from? Where are we going?* was still in pride of place in their New Zealand hall, and that it continued to amuse their visitors with its gauche jokes. I confessed to him the story of sitting next to Sam that night in Auckland, so many years before. He looked bemused, but I got the impression he was accustomed to the fuss over his younger brother, whom he has always called Nigel, his christened name. I also know that he gave Nigel/Sam a copy of my memoir, *Dadland*, and thinks if ever there were a film that Sam would be a brilliant elder Tom Carew. I agree.

And what a strange circular tale that would be.

THE CAMEL RAID

It began with desire. For a brilliant blue sky to flood the back of our retinas. But not to have to go too far. Then stars came into it. As many as possible. So it was that from a flat, grey, January London, we arrived in the small Tunisian town of Douz on the edge of the Sahara.

From the large flat roof of our pension we gaze across the town. Lucky, we think, to have bagged one of the only two rooms on the roof, each one its own entity, two small whitewashed cubes like sentry huts, with a window and a door. We gaze. Our view dodges through telegraph wires, along narrow dusty streets, past minarets, a glinting onion dome on the left, another further in the distance, and at the end of the street a silhouetted splay of palm fronds against the fading light of the shell-pink sky. On cue, a lone voice rings out in the call to prayer. The first star is out. We sense the sand. The very edge of it. Three million five hundred thousand square miles of it. A dry shifting sea. Dunes that rise like waves, up to 500 feet high. A landscape crisscrossed for centuries by the trade routes of camel trains, caravans of up to 12,000 strong, carrying salt and cowrie shells, bringing back gold, or kola nuts, or slaves. Tomorrow we will look for camels. Tonight we can only gaze.

At midnight, the occupants of the other room on the roof – our only neighbours up here – arrive. From the stampeding feet we calculate a dozen schoolchildren. We can hear the thudding of extra mattresses being hauled across the roof to accommodate them. We quickly revise our calculation: fifty schoolchildren. And their friends. The mattresses are not required, as the little buggers never go to bed. No matter, for tomorrow we will find camels to take us into to the Great Silence.

The next morning, bleary-eyed but breakfasted, we notice a sign down a narrow side street, chalked onto a board outside an anonymous door: Camel Raid. After a second of hesitancy, for it looks as if a child might have written it, we go in. Yes, they have camels available; yes, they have guides; yes, yes; one day, three days, a week. Yes, yes. Very nice camels. Very nice desert. Yes, they bring food. Yes, they have time to organise. Of course. Very good agency. No problem. Very good trip.

One instinct is to go with it. As though providence brought us here. A superstition about the importance of trust. Spurn this and it may mean bad luck. The other instinct is that maybe they have no camels; maybe this office is a moveable feast; maybe, after each booking, the chalk-written sign travels over to the next street. But they do have a photograph album on the desk which is full of pictures of camels and sand and the blazing blue sky.

We go with it, take the leap of faith, pay our money and book our *raid*. A week in the desert. Then have to resist checking out all the other Camel Ride establishments that suddenly seem to have sprung up on the way back to our pension. Proper offices with proper signs, and printed leaflets. Ours is more *authentic*, we try to smugly tell ourselves. More . . . Saharan. Not some regimented tourist itinerary. And how lucky now to have the day free, not to have to compare. Which would only result in terrible deliberations and indecision and endless discussion. Which would impoverish the day.

All day we see signs for Camel Rides, wherever we go. I can't help wondering. Out loud. I begin to worry about our *raid*, whether they have camels, whether there will be enough food. Whether we will ever see the organisers again.

At the appointed time of four p.m. we stand, crestfallen, in semi-disbelief outside the locked door, from which the Camel Raid sign has vanished. Then a horn blares at the mouth of the street. A young man in a long white *djellaba* and a midnight-blue *keffiyeh* gets out of a jeep. He beckons us over and introduces himself as our guide.

He is called Mohammed. We climb into the back of the jeep. There is nothing in the jeep. Except us. No provisions. No camel harnesses . . . And then, putting up a dust cloud, we are driven out of town, very, very fast.

Two miles outside the town, beside a crumbling ochre sandstone wall, Mohammed points to a pile of sacks on the ground, pulls over and skids to a halt. Beyond the sacks are two robed men holding three camels. Here, Mohammed informs us, is our camel driver. And here are our camels, two large ones and a baby one – which looks way too small to ride, and way too small to carry anything.

'This is Mansour,' Mohammed says.

The camel driver smiles, displaying a mouthful of broken brown crockery. One of his eyes rolls sideways and up, its pupil hides beneath the lid, leaving just the albumen, yellowing slightly, like an overcooked egg.

'*Sabah el kheir*,' we say, which we learnt at breakfast.

'And this is Zaid,' Mohammed says. We nod and bow our heads.

Mohammed and the camel driver talk rapidly together. I begin to feel a fluttering of ominous anxiety. Only two camels. Where were *their* camels? My smile becomes frozen.

Three of them and two of us. We couldn't possibly have paid enough money to hire *three* men for a week. And why only two camels? What if they mean to leave us in the middle of the desert and rob us? Or worse.

'Are there only two camels?' I ask.

'You need more than two camels?'

'No, but what about you?'

'We walk. You ride.'

'You walk?'

'This is normal.'

'Really?'

'Yes. Of course. This is normal.'

This is not what I had imagined. I had imagined three camels, three riders and a pack camel. A proper trek. Like a miniature caravanserai. I am worried. How far are they going to walk in the desert? It is hot. Bloody hot. And dry. And, I imagine, very deserty. Wouldn't they be very slow and wouldn't we have to keep waiting for them? Wouldn't they get so thirsty that they'd drink all the water? Do we have enough water? Where is the water? Who is going to carry the water? Let alone the food? And where is the food? What *is* in those sacks? One of them looks like a sack of flour. Why are we taking a sack of flour?

Nothing adds up. Now I am convinced we are going to be robbed. And left to die in the desert. The foolish tourists that we are. I remember *The Long Walk* by Slavomir Rawicz about an escape from a Siberian Gulag, when the seventeen-year-old girl, Kristina, was dying in the Gobi desert and how her leg went black first. And who would know? No one knows where we are. As usual, we have done no research, we know nothing about desert treks, we have just bought the cheapest flights and come. It is very possible that in all the guide books it says, *Don't go on a camel trek with a backstreet agency*. Maybe it says, *Watch out for conmen running suspicious Camel Raids*. Maybe *everyone* knows not to go to a backstreet agency, except us. And now, because we are too cavalier and too lazy and haven't got round to reading up about it, we are in mortal danger of falling foul of some heinous plot in the middle of the Sahara. The sign had said *raid*, after all. Couldn't we even read? I try to flash a look at Jonathan, which I don't want our 'guides' to see, but as usual he doesn't notice.

The camel driver meanwhile is busying himself with camel harnesses. Maybe everything is fine. These are honourable men, after all; men whose word is set in stone, whose unimpeachable moral standards put our debauched Western mistrust to shame. It would be unspeakably rude to back out now. Or then again, could we be about to die of politeness? I have been in trouble with politeness before. I look at Jonathan again. There is a plough mark down the middle of his forehead. I know that plough mark. He's not sure either.

'Do you think this is all right?' I whisper.

'What do you mean?' He sounds tetchy.

I believe his tactic is to make me feel it is ridiculous to worry about it, in order to make himself feel it is ridiculous to worry about it. My tactic is to make him worry about it.

'What happens if it's not okay?'

The camel driver is speaking to one of the adult camels as he yanks on its bridle. He thwacks it. It bends its knees and sits down. Then he does the same with the other and both adult camels are crouched down, chewing.

'Have you ever ridden a camel?' Mohammed asks.

'No,' we say in unison.

Mohammed laughs.

The camel driver and the other man start to load up the two big camels. One by one they strap the huge sacks onto the large saddle panniers, over the top of which they tie rolled blankets. It appears the two camels are doubling as pack and riding camels, which looks uncomfortable for us and doesn't seem quite fair on the camels. The camels chew thorns. The baby camel skitters about. Then the camel driver beckons us over. I am allocated the darker camel. I grab hold of the wooden pommel, navigate my leg across the saddle and inelegantly slide on board.

'Lean back,' Mohammed says. 'Lean back!'

Anyone who has ridden a camel knows what happens next. As the camel gets up, its back legs straighten and you are hurled forward ninety degrees while the front legs stay doubled up. There is nothing in front of you, for you are staring down the precipice of a long vertical scraggy neck that ends in a bony head full of long brown teeth that can chew thorns. You push yourself back against gravity with everything you can muster, because you don't want to be falling anywhere near the teeth of a camel. Then, suddenly, you are hurled back as the front legs unfold. And the camel is standing up. I look down. It feels like I am a very long way up.

I watch Jonathan hold onto his knackers as he makes a sort of cowboy noise while sticking his arm out like he's surfing a wave. The three men smile. And off we sail. Our kindergarten caravanserai. Two and a half ships of the desert. Mohammed walks in front, his white *djellaba* fluttering out, then Jonathan on his camel, then me, with Zaid and Mansour behind us and the baby camel running about all over the place. And so we lollop away from the town, into the desert. Into the 3.5 million square miles of sand crisscrossed for centuries by caravans up to 12,000 strong, carrying their gold and slaves and kola nuts. Whatever we are carrying, it doesn't look enough.

And my camel isn't walking properly. It's getting its stride all mixed up. Its legs are locked into the wrong order, and my insides are getting churned up. I try to correct it by putting all my weight over to one side, to make him change legs, like you do with a horse. But he just continues, his legs moving in parallel, front–right and hind–right together, front–left and hind–left together. This is ridiculous. Four legs work in a diagonal: front-right, back-left;

front-left, back-right; and so on. My camel must have got out of sync getting up, and now he can't sort his legs out. I shunt and shift and sway. My spine is undulating like a charmed snake. The cartilage is probably already popping out. Then I notice Jonathan's camel doing the same thing. And the baby camel. Ah . . . My camel doesn't walk in a diagonal like a horse, I slowly realise, because it walks like a camel. And so my mind is taken away briefly from our impending fate by the distraction of my spine getting accustomed to becoming a jellied eel.

The camels are slow. Astonishingly slow. Each step is deliberate, as each great camel foot splays out, taking the shifting sand in its stride. There is a meditative quality about this. I watch the feet of the camel in front of me. I ponder that it might make a good metaphor for a character in a novel, as supple and tough as the foot of a camel, as pliant and as unremitting.

'What's my camel's name, Mohammed?'

'Name?'

'Yes, name.'

Mohammed asks the camel driver. Mansour laughs, gesticulates. The white of his eye flips over. The camel doesn't have a name. It's a camel.

We continue to walk into the cool of the evening with the dunes giving way to patches of scrub. Our minds begin to stretch out like the landscape and the sky. The name *Sahara* is an English pronunciation of the word for *desert* in Arabic. Freya Stark, the first Western woman to travel through the Arabian deserts, lived for one hundred years. My first love was half-Egyptian, his family name, Badawi, meant *Bedouin*, he told me; his father gave me a book to read called *The Road to Mecca*, by Muhammad Asad. It was the story of a Jewish scholar converting to Islam in the 1920s, but the only bits I remember involved travelling in the desert, smoking hookah pipes in tents, the camels and the stars.

When we stop to make camp, we scout amongst the scrub for sticks for a fire. There's a surprising amount of plants growing in this desert, plants with very small leaves on dry silvery branches covered in thorns. Mansour hobbles the camels and unloads the provisions. One of the sacks *is* a large sack of flour. Mohammed lights the fire and we feed sticks into the crackling flames. Another sack is opened and it is full of raw lamb! Mansour undoes a saddlebag and gets out a large bowl. He piles handfuls of flour into the bowl, sits cross-legged, his white turban shining against the darkening sky, mixes the flour with some water and begins to knead. You can tell by the deft movements of his hands that he has done this many times before. Then he pummels the dough into a thick pancake. He rakes out some glowing charcoal embers from the fire and puts them in a small hollow in the sand. Then he simply places the dough on top, heaping sand over until he's made a small mound. We sit around the fire. Expectantly. We make small talk with Mohammed, a little English, miming, hand movements, a little French. Zaid appears to have come along just for the walk, for he doesn't seem to do anything. The amethyst twilight deepens.

Mansour cuts up vegetables, a carrot, onions, some lamb. The first stars pop out into what is now a royal velvet sky, pinpricks of light, one by one, more and more, until soon we are under a giant colander.

Mansour points to the mound of sand. It is rising. We watch. I place my hand lightly on it. Warm, rising, surreal, like the pregnant belly of a friend. It is breathing. We smile. The fire hypnotises us, its small flames leaping up like snakes dancing, and the sky grows deeper and darker and more velvety. We move in closer. Our faces glow copper. Then Mansour sweeps the sand off his breathing hill and scoops out the unleavened loaf. It's hot, he holds it on the points of his upturned fingertips, brushes off the grains from the crust, flicking at it with a rag. Mohammed dishes out the stew; Mansour breaks the bread. We are eager. We bite into the crust, releasing the sweetest, nuttiest aroma. We dip it in the broth of the stew. The lamb is the most tender, the carrots are the most sweet, the onions the most pungent.

We chew over and over. The crunchy crust, the soft rough dough, masticating slowly, like the camels with their thorns. Our world shrinks to the fire's circle. We sit on Mansour's blanket, sipping tea, while he crouches on the cooling sand. He pulls over a saddle to shelter us from the desert breeze. Our talk is simple, a lot of smiling, a lot of nodding, I hug my knees. We eat the sweetest, stickiest, most voluptuous dates I have ever tasted. And the desert surrounds us, the silence surrounds us, only the camels chewing, and the whispery fire. Slowly we forget ourselves.

We sleep around the fire arranged like the numbers of a clock. Mansour covers us with blankets. I feel like a child being tucked in. Weighed down by the blankets, I lie awake for hours watching the stars. So many it looks like a soup, or the light of an exploded eye, a fractal roundabout, a quillion tiny bubbles of silver light in a fizzy sky; no line could be drawn from one to the other, no unicorns, no crabs or bulls or huntsmen here, only the unending view of a billion billion years. In Spanish there is no word for heaven, only *cielo*, which we would translate as *sky*. Or *Paradiso,* of course, which is different, loaded. Or maybe I have got it wrong and they have no word for sky, only for heaven.

Next morning, after sweet coffee and dates, we set off before the heat builds up. Then Mansour suddenly runs off, his great strides kicking up the sand, his *djellaba* flowing out. He dives on something. Then comes back to us with cupped hands. We peer down. A pink nose peeks out from a halo of brown fingers. A jerboa. A kind of large mouse with long legs. He lets it go. It bounds away on its big hind legs over the sand. He laughs. A flash of crooked dolmens.

Mansour collects 'desert roses', the crystal spirals of amber petals formed by the wind and salt and sand, and puts them in our hands. He picks up fragments of Berber pottery. He asks Mohammed something in Arabic, Mohammed translates: *Very old,* Mansour says, *very old.* We gravitate towards Mansour. He sees things. Creatures. Needs. Moods.

At a desert well amongst some scrubby bushes we encounter a Berber group watering their sheep. Mohammed talks to them and they invite us to their camp for tea. We sip politely. Smiling, nodding, yet I feel voyeuristic, uncomfortable. An old man lies on a cradle. He is worried by flies. Mohammed asks if we have any paracetamol. Jonathan has a couple of aspirin. The old man swallows them straightaway.

The next day Mansour points to four tall palms in the distance. 'Oasis!' we hail excitedly, and make our way towards it. There is no visible water, but Mansour has spotted something. He climbs up one of the palms, unencumbered by his white flowing robe, and plucks from its heart a great big chick. An *enormous* chick. Fluffy and dishevelled, with long talons and a strong curved beak. He climbs down and passes the dazed thing up to me. There is a photograph of me on my camel holding this eagle chick, both of us startled, the chick's tufty down haloing its dinosaur face, my face smeared in white zinc, my battered broad-rimmed hat pinning down a thin red sarong decorated with Pacific Island dancing girls, which shields my neck from the sun. I look like the offspring of Miss Havisham and Steptoe. I don't know how I got to be so filthy. The horrified chick stares straight ahead. I pass it down and Mansour puts him back. But as we leave, a furtive discussion between Mansour and Mohammed breaks out. I ask what they're saying. Mohammed says Mansour wants to keep the chick to train him. It's worth money, Mansour says. Jonathan and I are devastated. For me, to take this lone chick would seed disaster for something much bigger. It would be an inauspicious portent which would stir up the gods. I see the parent bird's distress returning to an empty nest. The baby eagle in a cage in a dark room. Everything is so conspicuous here.

'Please Mansour. Don't take the chick,' I implore him. I am passionate. 'Please Mansour. Please promise, Mansour, you won't take the chick.'

I ask Mohammed to make sure he understands. I beg Mansour to promise he will not come back for the chick. He promises. I ask him to promise again. The chick must be free, I say. It would be bad luck, I tell him. I am suddenly full of gloom. I cannot bear that our camel ride should spell captivity for the wild infant bird. I tell Mansour it is very important to me. I press him to promise on Allah, on his children's lives. He seems unfazed by this. He promises. We head off. I look at him. He promises again.

We walk for four days. The undulating stride I've become accustomed to, a rough but regular passage; the dunes rising and falling away, rising and falling. The grilling heat. The brilliant blue that we'd longed for is almost monotonous now. At midday we hide from the sun. Mansour rigs up a shelter and hobbles the camels who browse the scrub. Zaid rarely speaks. He fetches kindling. Eats. Walks. As thin as a shadow. In the evenings we make camp. Mansour bakes bread in the sand and cooks lamb and peppers on the fire.

Sometimes Mansour sings, cross-legged, his body rocking, the broken ivories of his teeth bridging plaintive notes, desert notes that coil upwards. This is our life now. Walking, sleeping, walking, sleeping under the stars. Yet I am no wiser to the geography of the place. It slopes away from us, throwing out its own shadows, it shifts, and the only constant is where the sun rises and sets.

On the last day of our journey, the afternoon sky turns brown. A sickly cankerous glaze. Mohammed and Mansour walk on ahead. A light wind worries at their white cotton *djellabas* and flicks around their ankles. Mansour points to the east. The temperature drops quickly. Mohammed tells us we have maybe an hour before a sand storm kicks up. We find a hollow behind a ridge. Mansour and Mohammed work quickly, their *keffiyehs* wrapped over their whole faces, barely a slit for their eyes. Mohammed blue. Mansour white. They stack the saddles and provisions high to form a small wall. Zaid hobbles the camels. No supper this night. We get into our sleeping bags and bed down behind the saddles. Mansour puts his cloak over me. No, no, I say, for you. He shakes his head. Then covers us with blankets. We are completely cocooned. The wind begins. Slowly at first. Then louder and groaning. Sand blowing in, its fine dust everywhere. In our eyes. Ears. Noses. We pull a blanket tighter over our heads. The dark noise building, louder, relentless. And there we remain, a small huddle under blankets in the desert, being covered steadily by sand. A tiny dot on the globe in the vast ocean of desert, sand blotting out the sky, swirling and driving in. We are covered head to toe but still it gets in, the finest grains, rock dust, everywhere; small drifts build up over our eyebrows, around our ears, in our hair; even though we shut our eyes, it gets in, finds its way, scratching the lenses, collecting in the corners. Fine as ash, more and more, each wind-breath carrying the minute grains into our noses, restricting the air passage so we can hardly breathe. We cannot speak. We cannot sleep. Will the sand bury us? Where is Mansour? The sand keeps coming. The noise constant. All the long night, the sand. And the only noise the wind.

As suddenly as it came, it leaves us. We rise like moles. Blinking into the morning light. Heaving off the heavy blankets, tipping away the sand. Shaking the granules from our lair. Re-entering this world as if we had somehow been away. We look around and everyone is here. The camels dug in. Mansour dug in. Mohammed and Zaid dug in. We wake to a changed topography, to a hill that wasn't there before, and the buried scrub bushes. A dirtier sky.

On the last day, in the last hours, swaying on top of my great beast, I feel an unspeakable loss. When date palms appear on the horizon, I am silent. Everything that had been open and unprotected and borderless will be closed and protected and bordered. Our state of ceaseless wandering was about to cease. Our week – normal for Mansour, Mohammed and Zaid, but not normal for us. The wandering had become a connectedness. Our spines had settled into the camels' rhythm. We have been wrenched out of our familiar lives, and something has been soothed by the desert, by the silence, by the dependence on strangers. But now our no-man's-land is about to be full of people again. I know the town will be jarring. Everything will become more complicated. I ride behind the walking Mansour and watch the fluttering folds of his white cotton *djellaba*, his padding feet. We stop. The camels fall to their knees. We dismount. I have the hang of it by now, but I keep my eyes cast down because they are full of tears. We pat our camels as a jeep, in uncanny timing and like the enemy in victory, hurtles towards us.

We take Mansour's hands and embrace. His one eye bright, the other with its curdled yellow sheen. Mansour who had looked after us, caught us a jerboa, gifted us desert roses, baked our bread, put his cloak over me and put the eagle chick back.

'May God give you long life,' Mohammed translates for Mansour.

'May God give you long life,' we say back to Mansour.

Uncomfortably we press notes into his palm, swap addresses, promise to write. This time I will, I swear to myself. The jeep pulls up, spins round. Out steps the director of the agency to greet us, wearing a professional smile. We clamber in.

Three months later, back in London, the fax machine rings, and then groans into action. A handwritten message flops out.

Hallo my Dear Keeg

I hoppe that you're fine, and I want that you have spend a very nice Time on the desert. For me it was really a very nice Time With You and I want to see You another Time here in Douz. my best greetings. I want for a Fax from you.

your, friend,

Mansour

We imagine Mansour queuing at the fax office in his village and wonder who translated for him. It doesn't feel like Mohammed's style. We send back our greetings in large simple English. I post photographs to his address.

Hello Keeeg

I hope that you are fine with your husband jonathan.
Good life to you Both. I can't forget you but thse days
I have trouble in my life, because one of my camels
are dead days a go now and to work with one is like
nothing because the Agency prefer all the time people
they have two or more camels. and also I don't have
enough money to buy a camel. this is my problem now.
but you are all the time in the mind and in the heart.
Good luck for you Both. Have a good time. Write to me
Very Soon.

Your friend

Mansour

Which camel? What does a camel die of? How can a camel just
die like that? A rotten fist punches into the haloed memory of
a sacrosanct time. From the back of my mind comes a devastating
description of the death of a camel in *The Alexandria Quartet* . . .
something dreadful about its foot and its terrible screaming? I
try to look it up but can't find it. I feel uneasy. I thought camels
were tough. This is an awful fax.

'Do you think it's true?' I ask Jonathan.

'I don't know,' he grimaces.

Stupid of me to have sectioned the desert off from the rest
of the world. Everything dies, after all, or spirals down the
plug. Mansour, his camels, our seven days, I had tethered them up
in my *cielo* balloon. This is a spoiling blow, unbidden, the other side
of our experience with the place, and probably, realistically, the side

most intrinsic to it. We worry for Mansour. He isn't the go-getting type like Mohammed; we cannot see how he would fit in with the modern world easily, with its demands, or its sense of efficiency. He has a wonky eye. He is more comfortable in the ways of the past than the future. He frightens tourists. He'd frightened us. He had become a friend with whom we couldn't even share a language, but he had struck something essential. I seem to have invested a lack of my own into my vision of kinship with Mansour.

Dear Mansour

We are very sad to hear of the death of your camel. How did it happen? This must be a tragedy for you. We would like to help you with your trouble in some way. Please can you give us the whole picture so we can try to help? How much is a new camel? How much money do you have towards a camel? We send you all our good wishes and we will be in contact very soon.

Your friends

Keggie and Jonathan

We send another fax, to the director of the agency, to ask what has happened, and the following day receive a reply.

Dear Mrs

After your mail, took information about Mansour's Camels.

It seems to be the truth. The price of a camel is between:

800 and 1,000 DT. We cannot say more. It is a personal question. Hoping to see you once more in our desert,

Best regards

Mr P. Douz

Dear Keeg

Hello, I hope you are fine. About the camel, I have just 300 DT. I hope see you anther time in Douz. you are welcome.

Sincerely yours

Mansour

'How much is 750 dinah?' I ask Jonathan.

We check it out, 750 dinah plus commission plus charges costs £394.59. It is not much of a dilemma: Tunisian dinah in our world, in our lives, will soon be forgotten, lost and gained times over.

Dear Mansour

Thank you for your fax. If a camel costs 800–1,000 DT and you have 300 DT, then we will find 750 DT to help you. You now have to send us the details of a bank where we can transfer the money to you. Go and ask the bank in Douz and tell us where to telex the money. When you find a camel, tell us and we will send the money to the bank. Make sure the camel is friendly.

With best wishes

Keggie and Jonathan

Dear Keeg

Hello, I thank yo for your fax. About the information that you ask for:

I have bought a camel, that cost 1050 DT, it is a nice camel. My compte nember and address bank you will founded it in the second fax for this day. I hope that all be right.

Best wishes

Mansour

'That was quick,' Jonathan says.

'Yes,' I shrug. 'God knows . . .'

Dear Mansour

We have made a transfer for 750 DT to your account. It will take one week to arrive in Douz. With your 300 DT this will pay for your camel. We ask you three things:

1. Please give the camel a name.

2. Please never let anyone harm the camel, or eat it.

3. Please send us some photographs of the camel.

We hope the camel will be good to you (and you good to the camel!) We are very happy you have two camels again and we wish you peace and happiness.

'You can't write "don't eat the camel"!'

'Why?'

'Why would he eat the camel?'

'He told us. They eat camels. When they're finished they eat them.'

'If you give him the camel you have to *give* him the camel.'
'I know. But too late. I've sent it.'

Dear Keegi, Hello

How are you? I hope fine, I must thank you very well,
because I just receive your money, thank you very much.
I was in a big problem and you solve it thanks dear Keeg.
Dear Keeg, please choose the new name for my new camel
and I will have a big pleaseure if you can acccept invitation all come here To Tunisia and Douz to pass a trip in
the Sahara With my camal and me. You must be the first
to get on my camel and I will pay all the trip, Dear Keegi,
I hope that you accept, I want to thank you who help
me.

I will send for you photos of my camal. All my familly
thanks you very well,
BIG KISSES
Mansour

'Big kisses? I think he has a new translator,' Jonathan says.

We wonder who is writing the faxes from Mansour. I suppose
he addresses me because he must realise I write the letters, even
though I sign them from us both. We choose the name *Lily* for
Mansour's camel, after the newly-born daughter of friends. We
send drawing books and crayons for Mansour's children.

Dear Mansour

Hello! How are you? Thank you for your fax. We are pleased

to be lucky enough to help you get your camel. We are thinking of a name. Is the camel a female camel? How about Lily? If she is female we hope she will have many babies so that you will one day have a big caravanserai. We look forward to seeing you and riding your camel. Maybe next year.

Your offer is very kind and we look forward to coming to Tunisia again, and to meeting your family. Please say hello to Mohammed for us.

Our best wishes

Keggie and Jonathan

Hello, Keegi

We are fine and we hope that you also be fine. I and photographer, we will take photos of my camel (it's male) and my family, the name that you give to my camal 'Lily' is a nice name I love it, thanks. Also my children's was admire this name, now it's a official name for my camel. A day We (you and me) Will make a trip in Sahara With Lily it's a pleasure for me to be with you and visit Sahara. I feel so tired these days, because my wife was leave me, and I educate only my children and in ten days they will return in school. We are aspecting you and we hope seeing you quikly. Me and my family will be very happy to seeing you again because you are welcome at any time but just tell me when you will arrive to meet you in the airport. Please Keegi confirm me your arrive, I aspect you answer.

Bye, kiss

Mansour

'*You and me,*' quotes Jonathan, '*bye, kiss?*'

'Hm.'

Again, we wonder who is writing the faxes for Mansour, yet in the post he has sent us three photographs of a fine white male camel. Mansour proudly holds the camel, his three children are perched on top. He is scrubbed up, Western style, wearing a blue buttoned shirt, jeans with a belt. We hardly recognise him. Of course, we wanted a picture of him in the desert with his white *djellaba* and *keffiyeh*. We can see he has gone to a huge effort to get this photograph for us.

At Christmas we send presents for his children, stuffed toys, colouring books. On 1 January the fax machine grinds into action.

Dear Keeg

I you wish good annee. I have vecu a problem because my son Fathi have a accident in the house it be fall of roof of my house the night of christmas, the two foot be break, it have make a operation surgical have the hospital this operation be have the sum of 3500 DT maintenant I must pay the hospital but I be not this sum for that I be oblige to sell my camel which be my only means of travail. j'espere that you can we visit at me in my family je you wish a nouelle year full of joy. I think seriously to buy my camals to pay the doctor, how make operation for my child . . . after that immigrate to Libya; I am forced to do this solution and leave Douz and my familly. If you want to visit Douz, tell me I will stand you. I think you for present for my family sent by post, my children was very happy. thank you and hope to see you nearly. Je you wish a novelle year full of joy.

Your friend

Mansour

I was going to end the story here. Yet although we read this fax with a sinking heart it did not alter our affection for Mansour. We could understand. And then again, we had no way of understanding. We were just tourists on a bridge between cultures. We had already wondered about the translators helping Mansour, so we took the easy path and allowed a silence to fall.

Six weeks later the fax machine sprang into action again. 'My son feels good and my camels also, my work, everything is good,' reported Mansour, and we sent our love back in return.

At night, when I look at the stars, I sometimes think of Mansour. In the desert, cross-legged, his face copper in the light of the fire, a loaf of unleavened bread rising beneath the sand at his feet, his white *keffiyeh* so startling against the midnight sky. A tiny dot on the globe in the vast ocean of sand. And I wonder what became of him in all that has happened since in the Arab Spring that began so very close by.

THE ARROGANT POEM

Well . . . (Never start a story like this, and beware of parentheses, they draw far too much attention to themselves, apparently.)

I had been reading a lot of advice about 'writing' in books like *The Art of Fiction* (John Gardner) and *The Art of Fiction* (David Lodge); oddly these are the only ones I can find right at this moment on my bookshelf, but I remember accumulating various how-to books and practical guides about writing because *that* was what I really wanted to do. I had become the type of artist who when visiting a gallery spent longer in the bookshop across the road than looking at the art. For a start, writing was trans-portable; you didn't need a studio, or much equipment, you didn't constantly need to replenish (expensive) supplies, or frame the end result, or transport it, or store it. And a book cost under a tenner, cheap enough for anyone to buy. Nor did you have to go to a gallery to read it. You could take a book to bed and enter another world, like stepping into C. S. Lewis's wardrobe, into a world that could last for weeks, in a kind of one-to-one whispering, not the paltry few minutes one usually got being jostled along in an exhibition in front of a wall. I wanted to create the same heart-roar that I felt when I read things that lit up my interior world. I had been making art for years, but it was words, the eternal combustion of them, that gave me the giddy pilot-thrill of distant horizons. So I scoured articles and interviews with authors, searching for the Holy Grail, for the Secret (short-cut, more like), that would teach me about beginnings and endings and plot and structure and dialogue and character. There were a lot of dos and don'ts, with examples: 'get in, get out' (Raymond Carver), not what I'm doing here, obviously; 'unbloat your plot' (Colum McCann); 'never open a book with weather' (Elmore Leonard); 'keep your exclamation marks under control' (Elmore Leonard again!); 'do not place a photograph of your favourite author on your desk, especially if the author is one of the famous ones who committed suicide' (Roddy Doyle). The good thing about all these rules was that you were also allowed to break them.

So the toiling began. But in secret. Because I wasn't a writer, and apart from anything else, having avoided most of my school education, my spelling wasn't great, nor did I excel at grammar, in grammar, with grammar. When I should have been in my studio drawing or making up gesso, or thinking about my next exhibition, I was in fact not doing that at all; I was filling up notebooks with poems and phrases and stories and fitting the sounds of words together in ways I liked. Exercise books and jotters accumulated my scribblings – vital, I was convinced, for some future moment: 'cheeks as cool as cabbages', for instance; or 'feral moon spires of trees', whatever on earth they were. I looked west to America, to William Carlos Williams and Susan Howe and Charles Olson, and then back again to Samuel Beckett. I began to go to poetry workshops. I joined one poetry group in Kentish Town where we were given practical exercises, the first of which was in alliteration.

Astonishingly, in the ten or fifteen minutes we were allocated, as the competitive sweat broke out on my brow, I came up with a poem about wishbones. 'I have collected a kilo of wishbones, nearly,' it began. I mention this because it was an encouraging moment, for murmurings of approval gently ricocheted around the room, and I even felt a little bit pleased with myself.

Which is why I am now flicking through old notebooks and reams of typed pages searching for it, and the longer I can't find it, the more brilliant it becomes. 'Their bony bridged sternums' was in there somewhere, and 'linked like lures of lotto', and 'short straws', because it was some kind of metaphor for luck and hope, but also lucklessness, with the irony that the chooks whose wishbones they were had been roasted. But of course now I want it, it's not surfacing, which makes me *really* want to find it, so I am rummaging frantically through my drawers of scraps, I am trying to remember it but I can only resurrect snatches: 'each sucked spatula / gripped by finger and fumb'. Now, because I can't find the poem about the wishbones, it has taken on mythic status, and the murmurings of approval in Kentish Town have become gasps of admiration. And now I can't concentrate on anything else until I find the sodding poem. My whole shed gets a workover. I am completely sidetracked, for this wishbone poem is not even the poem I am supposed to be writing about. Nor is this: a tragic poem about a male parrot preening his feathers in the forests of Brazil, inspired by a radio report of a scientist, one Dr Cavas, closely monitoring the last known Spix's macaw in the wild, which had paired with a female blue-winged macaw. 'I am Spix Macaw / a solitary male / Oblivious to this fact and that . . .' I see I have just chopped it up willy nilly with line breaks of which I had absolutely no understanding. The parrot bows and flicks his wings, because *love is in the air,* but does not know, of course, how much hope is pinned upon the match, which 'could be enough to put a parrot off'. Alas, it did not turn out well for poor Dr Cavas, for both love birds disappeared; with them, the last wild Spix's macaw.

Flick, flick. I check the same drawer for a third time, but no wishbone poem; a story of a menopausal woman who puts a robin's egg in her mouth then swallows it; a story (typed on a Stone-Age manual typewriter with corrections xxx'd out) which begins, 'Deep, deep in the bowels of the earth, at the end of a very long cave, a mile from where the great seas batter the giant cliffs . . .' I have no memory of this story about a dragon who, due to his religious custom, takes his name from not just his mother and father, grandmother and grandfather, but a thousand generations before him, which amounts to more than a million names, which could be one way to fill a book, but luckily this dragon shortens his name to Humphrey. These sundry pages and torn scraps – 'It bites with stolen teeth' (I have no idea either) – are my vain attempts to plough my new furrow; but still the wishbone poem is nowhere to be seen.

The Kentish Town poetry workshop had spurred me on, but

each week the gruelling chore of having to listen to everyone else's poems, turn by turn around the room, with each week each poem getting longer and longer . . . well, it wasn't long before I gave up going.

Instead I bought poetry and writing journals (which I barely read) in which there were competitions you could enter, with prize money. £200, £500, £3,000! Imagine! The Biscuit International Short Story Award was £15,000! There was *Artesian*, *Ambit*, *Carillon*, *Mslexia*, *Mud Luscious*. I bought them all, paid my entry fees to the competitions and sent off my poems and stories. Into the thickening fog.

I never heard a thing from any of them. It was then that I came across one poetry magazine, *Quartos*, which offered a critique of the poem you entered into their competition, if you paid an extra £25 on top of your entry fee. By this time the encouraging murmurings for my wishbone poem seemed a long way back, and I longed to know if anything I wrote did anything at all. I selected my finest. A Beckettian (warning, warning) poem about trying to create a homunculus. I read it aloud and I liked the sounds of the hushing, and I liked the pictures and the hinting of things, and I liked the way it ended. And I liked its title too, 'A Ghost Story'. So I wrote out my cheque and I sent my poem off.

I waited. I imagined a real poet or a poetry critic reading my poem. Quite a long time later the envelope, addressed to me in my own handwriting, fell through the letterbox. Inside, there was a single-page generic critique form, with my poem stapled to the back.

My reference number was 566/P, which meant *Quartos* must

have had at least 566 other twenty-five quids, and one can probably assume that mine was not the last, so maybe they'd had
double that. A thousand hopeful wannabe poets out there, waiting
for their critique forms. Yet I could already see my critique had
scarcely been filled in: the first six sections were completely blank.
As I read the form my cheeks flushed with embarrassment and
my chest burned hot with confusion.

> This critique is aimed at giving some useful and
> constructive guidelines concerning material submitted
> for consideration in *Quartos* writing-related events.
> Time does not permit an in-depth assessment of each
> individual typescript but listed below are some of the
> pointers that might help with future submissions. No
> further correspondence will be entered into concerning
> the submission or the critique and the judge's/editor's
> decision is final. Nevertheless we hope this critique
> offers some valuable advice.

Beneath came a list of headings with a subset of questions, each
with a YES/NO to be ringed appropriately by the judge/editor,
along with your twenty-five quid's worth of criticism. Not for
me. There were no YES/NOs ringed at all.

Opening:
Is there a strong opening, introducing subject/char-
acter/scenario which makes the reader want to read
on? YES/NO

> Does the submission 'begin at the beginning' or
> waste time and wordage with preamble? YES/NO
> Suggestions for improvement:

All blank. I won't inflict my poem on you, but will just say my submission began, '*Yes a little creature / I shall try and make a little creature*' – straight from Beckett, but in italics to show I wasn't pretending it was my own. Anyway, no comment and no suggestions for improvement, either.

Middle:

Does the typescript maintain the reader's interest? YES/NO

Not ringed. I stared in disbelief, brow creased, shame puckering the inside of my cheeks. Surely 'I will burn with love and coo and coo / Who begat Who begat Who begat / YOU?' was a little interesting, and fractionally effective?

> Are there any superfluous details/characters, etc. which
> could be removed to tighten the piece? YES/NO

Fair enough, not applicable.

> Suggestions for improvement:

Blank.

Ending:

Is there a positive link with the opening? YES/NO

Yes, yes! There was 'Grey spew of an old man', which was defi-nitely linked to '*Yes, a little creature*', for God's sake. But zilch.

Has any surprise ending been used effectively?
YES/NO

Yes, yes, thrice yes! Shame was turning to anger now.

Was the ending predictable and/or easy for the reader
to spot? YES/NO

What? He (definitely a *he*, I had decided) didn't condescend to ring NO for even this.

Suggestions for improvement: of course blank.

Choice of Title:
Has the writer used imagination to create an effective
and eye-catching title? YES/NO

What was I to read into this? 'A Ghost Story' was at least a title, bad or good. I wasn't getting much for my money. Except that now my eyes were flickering towards the bottom of the page, skipping the 'Original thought/treatment of subject', skipping 'Description', skipping 'Narrative flow and pace', straight to the inch-wide box at the very bottom of the page: 'Any other comments'. Here there was a whole box full of handwriting. For it was here that something had snapped and my poet-judge had gone straight for the jugular; his handwriting stabbed the words into the page, upright and furious, as if he had written them with his fist:

My one complaint with this poem is its lack of accessibility. It's bloody arrogont [it is clearly spelt arrogont] to assume the reader can see your idea without any effort on your part, and you haven't made much have you?

I was being told off. My breath stopped, my skin cooled. I swallowed, my mouth dry with smarting humiliation. He wasn't finished, but he was running out of space, so the writing got smaller.

To be honest Plath on a bad day is better written than this.

And smaller, tighter, more urgent to squeeze in his final, all-knowing, damned-by-faint-praise, worse-than-anything killer blow.

However I've given you a B simply to encourage some more [sic] your vigourous [sic] imagery but [illeg., illeg.] with more attention to structure next time.

He knew, of course he did, that the patronising encouragement would be worse to read than the rage. Plath on a bad day? Plath on a bad day would be A+++, by my reckoning, for a lousy *Quartos* critique. And it is not like me to pick up on spelling – glass houses and all that – but this spelling was very bad indeed. This spelling was even worse than mine. And, I reiterate, I won't inflict the poem on you, except to say that 'I LOOK at you / clamp my mouth onto your cool fatty arm' surely is not a bad line – yes, why on earth put LOOK into caps, but I still get the temperature of cool baby flesh in my mouth when I read it. 'THUMBSUCKER', again in capitals, is a bit aggressive, I concede; and 'Looks like a severed head utteringobscurerhetoric' is possibly over the top; and 'masticating ivory mouth / nipping' is not very nice. Too much 'cooing' and 'skull-pounding', I admit. But what about 'Suggestions for improvement', what about 'useful and constructive guidelines' and what about 'we hope this critique offers some valuable advice'? What about my twenty-five quid's worth?

Thus I gave up entering poetry competitions. I stopped writing poetry; I would try fiction instead. I would write a novel about a son trying to discover the identity of his father, which his mother withholds from him. Three years later (not quite the 10,000 hours hard labour that Malcolm Gladwell posited was necessary to be expert at anything, but nearly), *The Dog Star* lay limp in the bottom drawer, with the reams of poems and short stories, and bulging notebooks and scraps. The wishbones weighed heavily. And as I try to wrap this story up, eerily prescient, and out of nowhere, the last few lines of the wishbone poem suddenly come to me:

gripped by finger and fumb the splintered sticks snap
and this kilo of potential
pulled and not pulled
turns out to be as lucky for me as for each cooked
chook that
bore its bone
for wishful thinking on its back.

THE INVISIBLE STORY

The email read: 'A giant, site-specific musical theatre event! . . .
developed by a unique creative team of storytellers, a composer,
a designer and an arctic explorer.' My friend had forwarded it.
She was going on a two-day weekend workshop as an experi-
ment – to help a scriptwriter resolve a difficulty with the script.
'A dynamic system,' the email went on, 'for revelation and
solution.' She was the invited composer, and thought I, as an
artist and keen storyteller, might be interested in taking part. I
scrolled down the list of the *unique creative team*. I had heard of
some of them – well respected in their fields. *An epic saga that
crosses the globe,* hmm. *Revolutionary*, I liked revolutionary. *A
unique and experimental event.* The email came just at the right
time. I had been working on my own for too long. I needed
to get out more. Interact. So I took it as one of those fortuitous
opportunities which every now and again presents themselves,
and said yes. Yes! I really should have paid more attention to
the blurb.

And so I arrive at the conference centre, a red-tiled converted mansion in north London where the workshop is taking place, early, brushed up, a little shy. Not wanting to appear too self-conscious I walk in breezily and head straight for the cafe and get a cup of tea. I sit near a friendly-looking group of older women who are already here. They smile welcomingly, and one of them moves her chair round to include me. Five minutes later, I realise I have mistakenly joined the Rebirthing Society. An omen perhaps. We laugh. I return to my tea, begin to read the email we were sent of *the story so far*. Which doesn't appear to have got very far at all.

A tiny doubt creeps in. No. Let me be as open-minded as I can. I am not going to jump to conclusions. Don't let me be the cynical person.

Thank God, my friend – and my connection to all this – has arrived. She is at the doorway, talking to someone she knows. I go over. She introduces me to the large, billowing, slate-blue silk shirt standing next to her, who is The Creator! and The Writer! We shake hands. But his eyes fall on something over my shoulder. The others. Almost thirty of us, including his *unique creative team*.

We sit in a large circle around the edge of the conference room, which has French doors leading out into a garden, and a Christmas tree in the corner covered in red balls. Some people seem to know each other. I sit next to a bearded young man. I turn towards him, hold out my hand and (accustomed to people calling me Peggy) begin to articulate my name clearly : 'Ke—'

He lurches back in shocked amazement. '—ggie,' I finish, disarmed.

His face relaxes into a smile. He tells me he thought I was

clairvoyant and was about to say *his* name, *Ke . . . nton*. We laugh.
I look around the group, twenty-eight of us. Old people, young
people, a long maroon skirt, a big flower on a t-shirt, a man like
a snowman with thick white hair, a man with a friendly face
who looks like a dog, a furry jumper, a leather jacket, dangly
earrings, a checked shirt, a big pendant, a head of pink streaked
hair, a woman wearing a headscarf tied behind her head like a
Dutch person. We are given an Aboriginal poem about a tree.
We all like trees, of course we do. We listen to a recording of
Joseph Campbell reading a speech from Chief Seattle.

The writer tells us he is The Writer! He introduces us to the
facilitator who is going to facilitate the workshop over the two
days and whom he says we are very honoured and lucky to have.
We introduce ourselves. It goes round in turn. Everyone is happy
to be here. *Very, very, happy. Excited. Honoured. An incredible opportunity.* Someone just says, *Lovely! Lovely! Lovely!* One woman shuts
her eyes as she speaks, reaching out with her hands as if searching
for the words; the ones she finds tell us that *anything* that addresses
what is happening to the planet, well, she *needs* to be here. There
are actors, writers, therapists, TV producers, artists, designers,
healers, a painter of butterflies, musicians, directors and a 'psycho-
synthesiser'. One person is called Myrrh. One person lived in
The Wilderness for a long time. *The soul is an organ of registration
of the body,* someone says. Another invokes the guardian angels of
the project. I am beginning to sweat. It is my turn. I say I am
happy to be here, then look swiftly to Kenton on my left. The
proverbial baton is passed on until each person has spoken and
we are back to The Writer! The Writer! tells us, 'This is, this is

not messing around with a play at the Royal Court, this is really, really big!' Most of the group nod.

The facilitator stands. A velvet scarf the colour of claret coils loosely like a well-fed python around her throat, the fat resinous beads of her amber necklace glint on her satin chest. Her voice is whispery, deep, earthy, rivery, all calm and willowy, her tonal moderation not up or down, but a steady middle note with little variation, slightly soporific. We are to call forth the soul's energies. We are told of the value and beauty in trusting our bodies. We are informed that 'Constellations' are sensitive to issues of Time and Space. We are instructed to surrender to the Truth of the Story. I look across the room to my friend, who is listening intently. Then the facilitator talks about ancestors and I find myself wondering if little insects are trapped in her amber beads, insects that might be a million years old, our minutest ancestors embalmed in sap turned to precious stone, nestled warmly on the bosom and in the vibrations of the rivery voice. Then she tells us to make a large circle of Time. From the oldest to the youngest. We each must find our place. And so we do.

The oldest in the group says he is depressed to be at the end of the circle: the end of his life. The younger ones rush to declare the respect they feel for their elders. I am reminded of what Jung wrote at the end of his autobiography: describing his feeling of advanced old age, he quoted Lao-tzu, saying something about all around him looking clear while he alone felt clouded. I decide to share this and make a hash of it. The facilitator gives me a withering smile – I've interrupted her. Too keen (desperate, more like), too quick, and anyway, it's not suitable. Wish I'd never said anything. I grope my way out. Now the facilitator wants a circle of *closeness* to The Project. We are to find our place again. The Writer! stands at the beginning of the circle. I am at midnight. Next to him. But on the wrong side.

'How does that feel?' the facilitator asks everyone.

Apparently, we have just *constellated*. Now we must *constellate* the story. Right. The facilitator places cards on the floor on which are written elements of the story. We are to walk around the story. As fast or as slow as we want. Let our bodies guide us. There is 'The Boy', there is 'A Secret' (but The Writer! doesn't know what it is), there is 'A Room', there is 'The Family', there is 'A Journey', there is 'Unhappiness' . . . Nothing is specific. Some of the story cards have question marks. The last one is blank with nothing on it at all. Right. So this could fit any story. Nothing about crisis, or consequence, or conflict, or climax. Nothing about . . . er, story? Okay. Slowly I'm getting it. It's a story without the actual story. Which is why we're here.

There might not be a story, but there is an event that sets off the story, actually not an event, a character – a boy, in a place, and he does something. The thing that he does – though maybe I shouldn't write this as it might infringe on The Writer!'s intellectual property – the thing that the character does . . . is to look into a hole. Now I think about it, I don't think I need worry about intellectual property, because a very long time ago, a character I created, called Muddle, looked into a hole. Muddle came from a children's book called *The Trouble with Muddle*, but this particular story was called *Muddle and Shrew Find a Hole,* and Juliet Stevenson read it on Children's Hour on Irish TV.

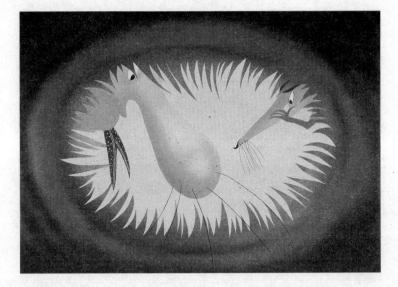

I made great big picture boards to illustrate the story and somewhere I have a tape of it. Proof, I suppose, so I think it's probably safe enough to mention that the main protagonist of this *giant site-specific theatre event* (exactly like my Muddle) looks into a hole.

We walk around the story cards. Then I notice that some people are hovering over the cards and deep breathing. Some people are swaying. The facilitator nudges The Writer!

This is obviously good. This is very good. The woman in the headscarf is guarding one of the story cards. She is standing astride it, not letting anyone get near. Her arms come out in a protective manner, encircling the space. Another person is rolling their head. The facilitator nods again to The Writer! While everyone is walking around the story cards in a clockwise direction, I am going round the story backwards. I realise I am being the cynical person, so I sit down. Then the facilitator makes us stand by the story card we feel most comfortable with. I stand by the blank card. Alongside The Writer! Is this good? I don't think so.

'How did that feel?' the facilitator asks.

'My knees nearly buckled,' says the dangly earrings.

'That was so powerful, so extreme,' says the furry jumper.

'My hands were tingling,' says a good-looking young man.

Headscarf tells us, with a frowning and intense expression – her pupils getting darker and darker and smaller until they are jet-black pins – that she was alarmed whenever a man came to the spot she was protecting.

'Yes, I felt the power of the feminine,' one of the men acknow-ledges.

There is a lot of nodding. Then we break for fruitcake and morning tea.

Twenty minutes later we are sitting back down in our large circle. Now we must *constellate* the story in greater depth. The Writer! prowls the room in order to locate his main protagonist. The Boy. He gestures towards the good-looking young man, but the woman who spoke earlier with closed eyes and outstretched arms, who *had* to be here, thinks he is pointing to her. Her hand is on her chest with overwhelming pride at being chosen. No, no, he does not mean her, he means the boy (I mean young man) next to her. She slumps back. The young man rises. The facilitator leads him into the centre, directs him *to find his place*. We watch. He moves right a bit, left a bit, here, no there, forward, then stops at the top of our circle, facing out towards the French doors. I am quite close, I watch him looking out to a distant horizon.

'Oh, and he has a dog,' The Writer! remembers.

The Writer! sweeps our circle, sees The Dog and leads him into the centre. The Boy tells us he feels much happier now his Dog is beside him. Now The Secret must be represented, so The Writer! lurches towards another young man, changes his mind and recoils away. He is sniffing, scouring – no, *channelling* – for his cast. I am channelling intently into my lap. The Secret is chosen. Then Nature is chosen. Leather Jacket is Colonialism, which later mysteriously and without a mention becomes Civilisation (no matter, but I thought that a very different thing). The Mother and The Father are chosen. The Grandfather is chosen. The characters are beginning to look like life-sized pieces on a chessboard. Two Grandchildren are chosen. The unchosen watch the chosen. There are now ten people in the circle. The facilitator and The Writer! walk around them inspecting them closely. The young stand with feeling and intensity. The older ones stand with seriousness. I am surprised how quickly everyone seems to have assimilated into this. Then I remember they are aspiring actors and wonder, meanly, if they are auditioning for a part in this *giant, site-specific musical theatre event*. But then I see that it is not just the young aspiring actors; *everyone* is standing with feeling and intensity. I am transfixed.

The facilitator asks The Father, 'How are you?'

'I feel great relief,' The Father tells her. 'Proud of my Dad,' he says, pointing to the Grandfather.

The white-haired Grandfather is so overwhelmed with tears that he cannot turn round. Bloody hell.

I look at my watch. We've only been *constellating* for fifteen minutes. Do they all know something I don't? I notice that Headscarf – the intense protector woman with the knitted brow, black pin eyes, and the scarf tied behind her head – has still not been chosen and is leaning more and more forward out of her chair. Oh dear. Headscarf says she *must* kneel, she has an overwhelming desire to kneel. She kneels.

Then Headscarf says, 'I need a connection. I need to do this together.'

Her whole body tips forward. She keels into the constellating area. The Zone. The facilitator hurriedly appoints her 'Ideology'. Ideology stands in front of Civilisation (who was originally Colonialism) and glares. After a bout of glaring she moves to stand behind Nature. The next time I look, Ideology is giving Nature a neck rub.

'What has been happening for you?' the facilitator asks Civilisation.

'My arm started swaying,' he says.

'What has been happening for you?' the facilitator asks The Secret. The Secret tells us she didn't want to be looked at. Didn't want to be *scrutinised*.

Hmm.

We break for lunch. My friend has disappeared to the loo so I gravitate to the woman who lived in The Wilderness. I want to hear about eating berries, watching bears, swimming in icy rivers.

'Where were you, when you lived in the wilderness?' I ask.

'In France,' Wilderness tells me. With her boyfriend, who was a terrible man, and a horse, and a donkey, and two dogs, a cat.

And probably a whole village, but I didn't like to ask. The garden outside the conference room has a bench under some trees. I take my apple outside. As I look up I see the remnants of a dead bird dangling from a branch. Another branch has snagged a sandwich wrapper. When I look back inside, everyone is beginning to sit down. I see my friend and hurry in, but there is no time to talk because we are having another debrief, and then, oh good, we will be *constellating* again.

Headscarf tells us how moved she was by the previous session.

A dark-haired woman in a long skirt says, 'I felt the power in the Tragedy of Time'.

The person next to her is nodding: 'I want to know something but I don't know what it is.'

I lose my ability to concentrate on the lulling voice of the facilitator as I am distracted by looking at everyone's socks, because everyone has taken their shoes off, and I am quite surprised at how many of their socks are odd. Then The Writer! is up, out of his seat, almost charging around the room, back, forth. He confirms his cast, The Boy, The Mother, The Father, The Grandfather, The Grandchildren, but now he needs a Grandmother. Yes! My friend!

Reluctantly she is beckoned from her seat. The Grandmother is blind . . . luckily. My friend stands stiffly in the circle with the other *chosen*, her cheeks pinking. I put my head back down to my notebook because I am trying to keep a nasty little smile off my face.

'We need Nature,' the facilitator coos, looking around for Nature. The Writer! beckons Nature to come forth again.

'We need Story, to represent all stories. The storyteller from the wise Inuit tribe,' the facilitator says.

And so Inuit is chosen – at last, the woman with the shut eyes and outstretched arms with veins rising to the surface, who *needed* to be here to address what was happening to the planet, who earlier had thought she'd been chosen as The Boy. She stands at the centre, tall, thin and rather lovely, with clear skin and long elegant fingers. The Grandchildren move towards her. They stand powerfully, expressively. But Inuit is already deep-breathing. Her arms begin to rise as if pulling the air into her. Now she is swaying. The swaying is getting stronger and stronger. Inuit is jiggling, the jiggling is getting stronger, more violent; she is now in a massive frenzy of movement. Nature begins to bend over like a snapped tree. The Boy, our main protagonist, who this story is about, is looking troubled. I look at my watch, we've only just come back from lunch. Nature is falling over. Do I sense some competition with Inuit? Nature, having fallen, lies broken for a moment. But not for long. Now she is crawling around the floor. There's a moan! It's Inuit. Inuit is now juddering *and* moaning. Grandmother's cheeks are reddening and she is getting stiffer and stiffer. Still juddering and jiggling and moaning, Inuit is now sweating, a snail-trail of shiny perspiration beginning to glisten above her lip. I can't see very well because the two Grandchildren are standing in my way. They hold hands. I have to lean round them to see Inuit, whose arms are leaping out, her fingers coiling in and out like a flamenco dancer's. The wooden floor is vibrating with her juddering. Nature has crawled over. She is beneath Inuit, looking up. Nature's hand is actually crawling up Inuit's skirt! I nearly burst out laughing. I roll my lips over tight.

The facilitator moves in, tells Inuit, 'We let you go.'

Inuit gasps then says, 'There's a . . . a . . . a . . . a story . . . crawling up my leg.'

That is *exactly* what she says. By now I know I must have an otherworldly look on my face. The facilitator looks down at Nature. 'We let you go.'

Inuit says, 'I'm going blank. I'm zoning out. I can't help . . . I can't help . . . I started . . . started . . .' she begins to swallow hard.

'Dying,' interjects the facilitator, nodding in a sympathetic way.

Inuit begins to slowly sink. Civilisation's arms begin to stretch out. And, oh no, Headscarf, who this time has managed to remain in her seat, is crying silently.

'I think something amazing has happened here,' the facilitator says.

'I think so too,' says The Writer!

I think so too.

At the end of the afternoon we go around the circle; each person is required to say something. A shy man begins to stumble over what is expected of him. The facilitator comes to the rescue by suggesting that he just wants to say thank you to The Writer! The shy man complies. It continues round the room.

'What has happened here today has been a powerful journey.'

'I feel overwhelmed with gratitude. Thank you for the generosity of the project.'

'I feel touched by a deep power outside of my body.'

Headscarf is too overcome with emotion to speak. She shakes

her head as little tears trickle out. This seems to have become a Feeling Contest. A sprint to the soul. Who can outdo whom.

'It feels like looking into the broken heart of the world,' someone says.

Top that! Someone does: 'What came out demonstrated that this was *a real situation*. I have done constellations with stories that did not resonate, they turned into very interesting intellectual exercises. But you can tell the stories that have some *balls* to them!' Laughter. 'Oh dear, a rather masculine metaphor. But this is one of those. This has *huge* resonance. This was a litmus test for your story. And your story seems to have passed!' Supportive group murmur.

My ears are popping. What story? What *is* the story? Where is the story? So far the story is invisible. Maybe *this* was The Secret. Maybe the story does not exist. It is a ludic puzzle or a Borgesian trick. Or maybe the story only reveals itself to the initiated. Maybe the words I was reading on the story cards were empty, while for the others the words on the story cards were pulsating and full of colour and, and . . . er, story. Maybe the story can only be revealed to a *real* prince, not frogs like me. Maybe real princes (oh dear, rather a masculine metaphor) know who they are, that their kiss will wake the princess, that their feet will fit the shoe, that they will wear the cloak of many colours. That must be it. Or maybe this is a great fat Emperor of a story with no clothes. I cough my thanks out as quickly as I can. We listen to some beautiful music. Headscarf is crying again – for the World. Then the facilitator tells us, looking meaningfully at Inuit, that tomorrow we will start at ten a.m., but to be careful when we leave because, after a highly charged experience like this, we might get run over.

I decide not to mention anything to my friend as we walk together to the tube; she is far nicer than me, not cynical at all, she is kind and supportive and trusting. And these were people she respected. She was excited by this project. She needed the work.

'What did you think?' she asks.

My eyes widen in a crazed kind of way. 'What did *you* think?' I ask her.

'*I* didn't feel what *they* said they were feeling,' she says in a baffled voice.

I hold my breath for a moment. Then tell her exactly what I think. Soon we are lost in hysterical schoolgirl laughter, about the juddering woman, and the moaning, and the falling on the knees. All the tension of the day pours away in a reckless rush.

'I am feeling my soul untied so that I can fly and feel the story enter the room,' I squawk.

'Powerful energies of the spirit engulf . . .' she chokes.

'It's . . . It's . . . It's crawling up my leg,' I explode.

'And it's a . . . a . . . a STORY!'

We go on and on. Exhausting ourselves. Until the tube pulls into Bank, where we go our separate ways. I keep bursting into spontaneous laughter on the walk from Liverpool Street Station all the way home.

The next morning I arrive a little late, and sit across the room from my friend in one of the two remaining seats. I make a mental note not to catch her eye. I look around the room, then it dawns on me that the one empty seat is Inuit's. The woman who was juddering and moaning. Maybe she did get run over? I look around again. No, Inuit is not here.

Now we've slept on it, we each must say something about our experience so far. Luckily I am almost the last. The man at the beginning, in a checked shirt, with grey hair, says he is disturbed by the loss of Inuit. The facilitator and The Writer!'s heads swivel round. They look left, right. They hadn't noticed. They see for the first time – no, she is not here. Where is she? But wait, Wilderness has her phone number. Wilderness punches the keypad on her phone. We wait. No reply. Because her mobile is switched off. A ripple, like wind across a field of wheat, rustles through the group.

We forge ahead. Minus Inuit. Now we've slept on it we are *overwhelmed, moved, deeply moved, bowled over, in awe, energised, astonished, transported; it was an honour, it was the birthing of something new.* One man had a dream last night of blind children eating bread, to which a woman with red hair observes, 'The earth is trying to tell us what the story is.' Headscarf says she felt *respect, and deep, deep gratitude.* Then Butterfly Man says he is *concerned about the story.* The Writer! looks darkly out of his seat. Quickly on to the next person, who says it is like the constellation workshop she did last weekend (constellation junkie), and she is struck by *the power of everyone and everything having a place and being seen in that place and, er, a very strong resonance.* Myrrh says it is *something big and vast and way beyond words.* Then my friend confesses that she did not feel the emotions to the extent that the others seemed to have done. The Writer! fidgets in his seat. Next person. Who is *in awe* of people's *authenticity,* and *bowled over by how people showed that, er . . . really instantly.* Me too.

Nature gives a long speech, her hair scraped back so tightly it looks as if there are claw marks round her head. 'This is a deep-heart place, which feels very fragile and um, vulnerable but it seems important to find a voice for this place.' She explains how historically she has always spoken from her mind, but now real-ises it's safe to speak *from this place*, she touches her heart. 'And it's about every aspect of life,' she says. 'And when I was being Nature I really felt this difference when my heart expanded, and then it felt very suffocating and I actually felt my heart was suffocating. All last night, I was just trying to find it, trying to find my breath,' she breathes in deeply, 'the breath of life, and that is something, as well. Um, and just lastly to say, there is something about, um, the power of the collective and that voice, and the channelling, and the power of collective channelling. And the channelling feels really powerful, um, yeah.'

There are more revelations and soarings into the stratosphere, and delving into the deep layers of the psyche; someone describes the process as a *sacred marriage*.

Then, oh fuck, it's my turn.

I hold my breath a moment, then say, 'For me, the jury is still out.' Silence. Then I say that I think some of the declarations of . . . er, feelings seem a bit . . . heavy. And, er, a bit premature. And taking courage from Butterfly Man, I add, 'And I'm a bit, er, worried about the story . . .'

The Writer! stares coldly at me from across the room. Then jumps his eyes quickly to the next person. Who says she was *bowled over by the power of yesterday*. She reminds us she's already described it as *Fierce Love*. 'Yes, that's the phrase still in my mind,' she says, 'Fierce Love.'

Then Wilderness rushes from the room with her phone pulsing.

Wilderness returns a few minutes later to tell us that Inuit felt fractured after yesterday, and that she had . . . *blown apart*. But Wilderness has persuaded her to return so we can heal her. The facilitator nods sympathetically. She knows we are all concerned, she says, but she has watched people fall apart and then come together again, in ways they are very glad of. The Writer! is *particularly concerned!* And *moved* by our comments. Although, he says, he found *the critical voices* very hard to hear. He loved whoever said it was a *sacred marriage*.

'That was beautiful,' a voice agrees.

And here we all are trying to find The Writer! his story, and The Writer! declares this is *revelatory* for him, and *transformative*. He is experiencing *a fantastic liberation*. He tells us his characters are becoming fuller and more rounded and more complex. Far from the cliché characters he had first written.

'For instance, The Mother and The Father crying and looking for each other; that's so deep and so much better. And the story is coming and coming. And then, someone said, "We haven't discovered the secret," and I went, "Shit!"' Everyone dutifully laughs. 'And then they changed it and said, "Or it hasn't revealed itself". It was wonderful you said that. You changed criticism into something affirmative.'

The woman in question leans forward. 'It's so clear the story exists, and you are just apprehending it in a rather mystical way. So you don't have to worry. It's so powerfully here.'

Then The Writer! tells us how amazed and *astonished* he was when Civilisation started to melt. 'That was so powerful.' He says he is also aware that he must remove blame.

'We can't have blame. Blaming one generation for all the problems in the world. If we fall into blame then the story can't move on. This catastrophe we are trying to deal with; to, er, heal . . .' he says.

I pitch in. 'I'm not sure I agree with that,' I say. Everyone turns round.

'If blame is surfacing,' I suggest, 'then maybe that is the tension you need . . . or something like it . . . to move your story on. To create a tension, surely the conflict is necessary . . . to be resolved, or . . . or the story isn't really a story.'

'You sound just like a producer,' he snaps.

'But it's true,' I persevere, 'or the story will be bland and dull.'

A thundercloud falls over his face.

The words *dull* and *bland* inflate like great balloons, filling the room, then reverberate into great whoopee-cushion words, polluting the atmosphere, infiltrating into every crevice. Bland and dull! Oh yes, I now have a part. I have cast myself. I am the three-headed, fork-tongued Hollywood-devil producer. My friend's cheeks are two very bright pink cushions either side of her face.

The facilitator steps in. She doesn't want this to turn into *a multi conversation*, she says, because we have the constellations to do.

'I don't think it is our job to worry about the story,' she tells us. 'Michelangelo's *David* was waiting to be hacked out of the rock. The cost is a lot of grief. The situation . . . the story is catastrophic, and there is no cheap way to hold catastrophe. One day is a short time to finalise anything about the state of the world.'

The Writer! nods solemnly. So that is what we are doing. Finalising the state of the world. I really should have paid more attention to the blurb.

Then Inuit walks into the room. Inuit's face is white, porcelain, gaunt. She has a beautiful face, but everything has been stripped away except pain and grief. She stands in front of us. Summoned back. A spectacle. Naked devastation. Everyone goes quiet. Tears begin to stream down her face. She stands rigid and tall. We wait. She is trying to say something.

'I just need . . .' She gulps in air. 'I just need . . .' She looks around the room. 'I just need . . .' Her eyes open wide. 'Love,' she says.

I swallow; my saliva tastes like dead frogs. Did I hear that right? The moment is gone and I can hardly ask. The facilitator takes her by the hand and leads her into the centre of the room. She is a windsock apparently, and we must clothe the windsock. So The Dog and Nature are led in to hug her. They hug. We watch. Bloody hell.

Then we break for coffee. My friend looks a bit cross. She tells me that I was a bit . . . fierce, and that The Writer! is very sensitive to criticism. I say I wasn't fierce, I was not criticising. Her face tells me she thinks I was. Everyone else is talking and bonding. Nobody will catch my eye. I go up to The Writer! and tell him that I am not a Hollywood producer.

'You sounded just like one,' he says. 'What you said was exactly what all producers say.'

Headscarf is standing beside him looking concerned and deep. Her eyelids flutter. I will not look at her. I say I did not mean to sound like one, but that *I was just trying to engage in the process, and er . . .* I stumble over my words.

The Writer! tells me I no longer sound like the person I sounded like in the room. He spreads his arms out and says, 'Let's hug.' His knee-length shirt unfurls. Gravity pulls my body in towards the chasm. Inescapably, I touch the silk. We hug. A terrible Judas hug. A stage air hug. A great lie hug. He turns immediately away. I hate myself. And now I hate him.

Ten minutes later we are back in the room, constellating. All the Ancestors are being chosen and lined up. Future ancestors and past ancestors face each other in a long line.

Right in front of me like a great wall. Almost everyone is needed. Not me. In spite of the hug, I am The Producer. The fault-finder. The unconvinced. The infiltrator. The impostor. I am the cynical person. They know.

The facilitator tells one of the Ancestors to say, *I lost you but now you are back.*

'I lost you but now you are back,' says the Ancestor.

I agree to this place, the facilitator directs another.

'I agree to this place.'

I move seats (everyone's seat is now empty) to get a better view. The Mother is purposefully not looking at The Father again. She glares at him, seething with hatred. Then she looks away. Then back, glaring with hatred. Real hatred. She tells the facilitator she is angry with him. Her look is frightening. The Father looks confused, and genuinely hurt (after all, he doesn't know her).

The facilitator leads her away. 'Tell your husband, *I got too big.*'

Long pause: 'I got too big.'

The facilitator asks The Father, 'What does that feel like?'

'It almost knocked me over,' The Father says.

Meanwhile, The Writer! is whizzing around the room, observing the scene from this angle, from that angle; he leaps on a chair, looks down on everybody, gets down, looks up. And then I see The Mother's bottom lip trembling. Her face begins to crumple. Oh no! It is The Mother's turn. The floodgates open. And the crying very quickly turns into a long, loud wail. She wails. And wails. And wails. Her wail becomes so loud and earth-shuddering it reminds me of the moment my mother died. My real mother. When something rose up inside me and I wailed from that deep unfathomable place something that encapsulated all the years of her life ending, her long road, her hard travail; and everything we had been through flooded back with the finality of never seeing her again.

But no one has died here. We are in a room. Then I see a hand coming into the circle towards The Mother, and at the end of the hand is a white tissue. A tissue! *A tissue, a tissue,* someone is giving wailing Mother a fucking tissue. She needs a bucket.

I cannot go on. The blue sky through the window is pulling me outside. Not even my curiosity can keep me here. Not even the spectacle of this story. We break for lunch. The tables fill quickly. I hover painfully on the edge. My friend is talking to Kenton. I tell the facilitator that I am not coming back. She smiles. She says she is sad I am not coming back, but her look tells me she knows my kind. I am the blocked person. As I nod my goodbye, my eye snags on the amber beads, looking to see if there are any trapped insects.

I walk towards home across the Heath. The long way round, past *real* trees. Then I catch the tube at Kentish Town. My friend later tells me that Inuit slept the whole afternoon, curled up in a nest they made for her, in a protective bed of coats and hats, beneath the Christmas tree.

THE CONSTANT MURDERER

All gardeners know gardening books are full of lies, but I didn't know the whole garden was full of deception. I'd thought of the garden as a place where one could lose oneself in contemplation, or in the physical labour of tilling the ground. *To be close to nature.* I felt that longing for the numinous breath, for the epiphanic moments at dusk, for the night sky. To inspect the minutiae, count the velutinous copper freckles in a foxglove's throat, or lie beneath a great ash and let one's eyes dilate, wander upwards, fuzz out into the spangled blue. Birds sang in gardens and built their nests, flowers bloomed and perfumed the air. Blossom after scented blossom. I longed for a garden of my own.

I *needed* one. I'd become deranged. I'd go mad if I had to write one more letter to Tower Hamlets council complaining about the pimps on the corner of our London street, and the perma- nent *bleep bleep bleep* of the fork-lift reversing again and again *all day* outside my window *for the last six months*, and the extractor fan on the roof of the new catering company chugging out its warm cabbage breath at fifty decibels. Not to mention the crazed two a.m. drumming from the Celestial Church of God in the warehouse over the road, and the all-night *thump thump*, *whirr whirr* of the sweat-shop sewing machines laboured over by the poor slave-workers going full tilt next door. (Noise and guilt!) Or Bob Pyke celebrating *another* windfall after hiring his basement out again to *another* film company by having *another* party with the doors open into the light-well so that all the noise flooded up, adding to the sewing machines and the crazed drumming and the extractor fan. And every day said film company replaying the same moronic phrase of the new *Atomic Sexpot Psycho* music video they're shooting in our road, which they're blocking with their generators and wind machines and catering vans and skimpy models and cables everywhere as fat as your arm and hordes of people just standing around *telling you you can't walk down your own frigging street*. The street that, I'm told, with the addition of a fake fire hydrant or two, is one of the few streets in London that can pass as New York. Not for me, sadly, the satisfaction of outsmarting them, like my clever neighbour Adam, opposite, who set up a row of teddies in his window to undermine the street's credibility. That clever Adam, he blagged a whole case of Moët in exchange for taking the teddies down.

Not me. I was just losing it. Fuming and festering and writing long potty letters of complaint to the Environmental Services. They knew me. But the day their telephone number came up as *Friends and Family* on our BT account I knew it was time to go. Time to stop fighting. The plane trees (annually threatened by the council because their roots might be interfering with underground cables, *EVEN THOUGH THE ROOTS HAVE BEEN*

THERE FOR DECADES!) would have to take their chances without me. I was done in. Beaten. I needed a garden. I *NEEDED* a garden. And then we found one.

One six-hundred-millionth of England. Half an acre. With a tiny cottage attached. So we moved. To the country.

So, hooray! No more reversing-forklift bleeps. No more two a.m. voodoo knees-ups. No more film companies. No more thrumming sewing machines and middle-class guilt. The odd helicopter, the odd (and very annoying) microlight going round and round in the same blasted place right over my head. And one bird in the *unbelievably early* dawn chorus sounding remarkably similar to the single-noted reversing forklift truck. But finally, earth beneath the fingernails. Edward Thomas in 1915 said he had fought in the war 'Literally, for this'. He rubbed it in his hands and let it sprinkle down. The soil. The medicine of it.

I rubbed it in my hands, and then went and bought some books to read up about it. Gardening books. Gardening books! The sweet-scented promise of all that was to come. I could make plans. Plans of arbours and gazebos and shimmering mirrors of water with lilies and autumn leaves floating on them, and twining honeysuckle, and garden seats around trees, and orchards, and urns, and jasmine, and dark yew hedges with arched doorways, and unexpected vistas, and spindle spinnies, and sundials, and spires of hollyhocks and foxtail lilies, and herb knots, and weathervanes, and nesting boxes, and scented night stocks, and more arbours, and rose bowers, and espaliered pear avenues, and camera obscuras, and moon gates, and quince loggias and sheds, and more sheds. And, oh yes, we wanted anemones in drifts.

Except. Gardening books are full of Latin. It hadn't occurred to me I would have to learn another language. A language of names. Unpronounceable, unrememberable, unlearnable names. Because when you look up sweet pea, it says 'see *Lathyrus odoratus*'. So from S you must flick back to L, but by the time you are halfway down the L column you have forgotten what the name is – *Lithriyinithiunus* or *Lyithrusys* or *Lthryayus* – and have to go back to sweet pea again to find *see Lathyrus odoratus*, and back to L, again. So many good gardening hours wasted, prodding Latin words in the index – always in italics, which makes them harder to read, which is why you have to keep your finger on them. And I'd also like to know why the sodding index goes to all the trouble of telling you to 'see' something with about thirty unreadable letters in it, when it could just tell you what page it is in the first place, which would take up less ink. Lily of the valley, see *Convallaria majalis*. Red-hot poker, see *Kniphofia*. *Eupatorium maculatum atropurpureum* (try that!) is Purple Bush. *Eupatorium purpureum* – Joe Pye weed. From Latin to Cockney, it seems. *Joe Pye*. I prefer the vernacular. Names like bastard toadflax, lady's bedstraw and codlins and cream. The hyphenated: touch-me-nots and forget-me-nots, Jack-go-to-bed-at-noons. And all the worts and spurges and greaters and lessers and creepings and hairys and sweets and stinkings and rues and bills and vetches. Oh, the names, they sent me into dreamy reveries.

And if flowers were good, I was soon to discover that the names of moths were even better. Straw belle, toadflax brocade, speckled footman, the buttoned snout (*oh, oh!*), the drab looper, the barberry carpet, mother shipton, the puss moth, the garden tiger, the pretty chalk carpet, the bulrush wainscot, the clouded buff, the true lover's knot, the ghost. The male ghost moth is bright white and gathers in large groups at particular spots, in a meadow for instance, to attract a mate. They hover together and gyrate, swaying from side to side in a peculiar motion called *pendeculating*, their eerie shuddery whiteness shining in the moon. Pictures of moths mating look like Rorschach blots. Their union is end to end, joined at their last abdominal segment. And their wings touch, tip to tip. Two thick furry cones locked together like a docking exercise for military hardware. I like moths. And I like the word. Moth.

'Did you know,' I asked Jonathan, 'that moths make up 97 per cent of the order *Lepidoptera*, with butterflies making up the remaining three?'

It didn't surprise him, he informed me (he likes to think he knows stuff about The Natural World).

It seems that moths, as opposed to their glamorous cousins the butterflies, are not appreciated as much as they could be. But they have nicer antennae, for instance. Unlike the clubhead on the end of the antennae of the butterfly, some moths have feathery affairs. Like TV aerials. For smelling. And, unlike butterflies, they rest with their wings open. So you can get a good look at their camouflage. Their woody barkiness. Their lichen mimicry. Or their resemblance to bird droppings. Or a second set of eye spots. Or toffee marbling. Or a fake mud-crack fissure of zigzags. Or simple fuzz. But the thing about moths, for a creature so good at deception, is that they completely blow it when it comes to light; spiralling inwards, they come back and back, bashing into it, singeing their papery wings, embalming themselves in the wax pools of our candles. Hardy's envoy from Wildeve, in *The Return of the Native*, was a premonitory moth which perished in the candle's flame. Mysterious pagan night creatures. And a literary device.

It is not only the names that are Latin. Colours and shapes, and geographical origin, are Latin too. I'd begun to learn a little by now: *nitidus* is glossy; *alba* is white; *virgineus*, unblemished white; *papyraceus*, paper white; *cretaceous*, chalk white; *melleus*, honey yellow. A greyish whiteness caused by hairs overlying a green surface is *canus* or *incanus* – that is what the book says: well, which one is it? A marigold cannot be a marigold, it is a *Tagetes*. There's always the exception, of course. These index editors are perverse: 'Sweet pepper, see *Peppers, sweet*'. Aargh! And no Sweet Williams at all, which is a pity, for my mother grew them and their scent takes me back to our small brick-walled garden in Fareham High Street. She trained fruit trees in fans against the wall – I remember that wall; warm, old brick, with its madder reds and clay oranges, soft and rounded; and my brother Patrick climbing it, for some reason always in a Viking helmet with plastic ox horns. It's all coming back – I remember the asparagus bed, a giant bare grave out of which those scaly, green armadillo tails poked up each spring and then disappeared. We never knew where they went. I never tasted asparagus when I was a child, and now, after our first crop, sweet nectar of the gods, I know why.

Crop. A rather violent sounding word. According to Jonathan we were now cropping. Beetroot for instance. Beetroot, how extraordinary, when you look at it, when you think about it. I mean the alchemy of it. A tiny dry seed transmogrifying into such a bright juicy bauble. I told Jonathan it was like the Big Bang in miniature. He was digging, he was un-riveted by my Big Bang theory. Blake, of course, had his grain of sand, but I am thinking (visionary as he was) that my beetroot is better than his grain of sand. A grain of sand is too barren – I *know* that was the point, but rather than stretching the imagination, I think the choice of sand limits it. However hard I try, I cannot really get going with the sand metaphor. No roots, no leaves, too uncon-sumable. *To see a World in a Grain of Sand* . . . I would go as far as to say you can't. Unless of course we'd already got to Armageddon. To See a World in a Globe of Beet. There. And I think you could see heaven in it, too. But more importantly, and more to the point, like everything else, a beetroot *dies*. And so the dying began. Death entered our garden (as if it hadn't been there before) with knobs on.

The first gruesome casualties (well, obviously not the very first) were taken by the chicken-wire over our thatched roof – which is there to stop the birds getting in and making holes in the straw. I just happened to look up. Three – no, four! – fresh baby sparrow corpses trapped under the eaves. I couldn't work it out until I saw there was a nest in the straw where the wire had reared up, enabling an entrance into the thatch. The fledglings on their first foray must have taken a wrong turn. A doomed peregrination under the wire. We untangled the dead birds and stitched up the entrance to the nest.

Then, oh, oh, a couple of days later, in the same place, I heard an insistent *peep peep* and saw another fledgling trapped. And another further up. And just beside it, its dead brother, and then another closer to the nest. I ran around beneath the thatch panicking. We had unwittingly closed up the wire on a second brood. I sent Jonathan up the ladder again; he cut the wire, and herded the birds by prodding through the chicken-wire with a broom handle. They headed off further into the thatch. One going this way. The other going that. *No! No!* Desperation engulfed me. I screamed advice from below. We decimated the wire until eventually all three baby sparrows teetered on the edge. Then fledged.

The demise of the baby sparrows that didn't make it chilled me; it sped me back once more to Fareham, to a memory I'd buried long ago, when I was in the habit of stalking fledglings around the garden with a blue tin of Saxa salt. I had been duped by the old-fashioned illustration on the tin of the long-legged boy sprinkling salt on a bird's tail. This was what one had to do to catch one, apparently. I spent hours chasing hapless thrush and blackbird babies around the garden until I cornered a fledging sparrow one day and it hopped under a gooseberry bush. I got down with my big kid's head and peered under the bush and met a beady eye. Oh, the hunger to stroke it, to hold it in my hand, to prove to it I wouldn't hurt it, to prove to it I would set it free (after I had mauled it good and proper, no doubt). It *needed* to know this. I tipped out the whole contents of the salt tin but no bird hopped out of the bush. As I poked away with a long stick, it edged further in. For hours I tormented it, or whatever hours are for a five-year-old child, and then got bored. A week later I happened to look again. The dried-out feathery husk of a baby bird was trapped exactly in the last place I'd seen my baby sparrow. My heart plummeted and my skin went cold. I had forced it in there. I'd killed it. I had blood on my hands. I tormented myself: why hadn't I gone back to check? Even now I can see the vicious spiked branches criss-crossing over the poor bird's body, its beak pointing upwards, its shiny eye closed.

There were to be a lot of tragic bird deaths and inadvertent killing in our new garden. The blackbird in the rat-trap, for instance. The trap had been set inside the garden shed, but the door had been left open and the curious bird (a bird in spring is a busy bird) had discovered the cheese and pecked it. The next time, Jonathan hid the trap behind shovels. And caught the blackbird's wife! I know it was his wife because their newly fledged child came looking for them, *beep, beep, beep.* All afternoon it hopped and squawked and squawked and hopped, *BEEP, BEEP! Beep, beep, beep*, which we grimly understood meant: *Where the hell are you?* The loss of one parent is unfortunate but two is fatal. So the baby blackbird – we named him Harry – was taken in. And our worm composter came into its own. Worm after worm after worm slipped down Harry's bright yellow throat, writhing clusters of them, miniature Gorgon's heads. I held them up, his reflex trapdoor opened, glug, glug. The almost cartoonlike dazed eye. I imagined the worms inside, still wriggling surely. Soon Harry was busting out of his box in the kitchen at night so we began roosting him in the hedge. Before six in the morning he'd be at our window for his breakfast, *beep, beep, beep,* our very own reversing forklift driver, *beep beep!* He woke us up and we couldn't ignore him for he was hungry all day long, following me around, *beep, beep*. Or flying at me in the garden, then landing on my head or my shoulder; if I put my arm out he would land in the palm of my hand. Little children would come from far and wide to visit Harry. And of course I began to love him. Which meant I began to worry about him. I couldn't go out for longer than an hour at a time. Rushing back for Harry. So I began to teach him to get his own worms.

Together we foraged in the flowerbeds, but by now it was obvious, with his speckledy chestnut breast, *he* was going to be a *she*. And then she got a cough, actually more like a sneeze. I rang the RSPB and they told me that hand-reared birds were prone to this and suggested some cough mixture, and so I administered the drops. *Beep, beep*, sneeze, sneeze. Oh, my baby bird.

And then my nephew and niece came to stay and we didn't see Harry again. I like to think Harry chose bird-dom, but I don't think she did.

We stopped setting traps after that. And became infested with rats. They climbed the apple tree and swung off the peanut feeder. Congregated happily on the bird table. Big ones and their babies. Country rats, fat and field-wise. Then the rats began running across the cedar shingles of the kitchen roof. Larking about, even, on the lawn. I was frightened for the birds' eggs. And the fledglings. And us. So the rat-catcher came. The sole arsenal of the rat-catcher these days – as the law dictates – is anticoagulants. So the rats must haemorrhage from the inside. Slowly and painfully, they staggered about. Bleeding rats everywhere. Swaying in a tormented stupor until they finally keeled over. Unless Jonathan could thwack them on the head with a shovel. Oh God. No more rat poison. Which was when Jonathan said, 'We'll get a gun.'

Hang on a minute. *We'll get a gun?* A year in the country and we're getting a gun? The whole idea was to *live* with nature. Not obliterate it. I don't kill things. Well, I try not to kill things. I only kill things by mistake. Even insects. *Do not harm the fly, he washes his hands, he washes his feet.* Learnt by heart, taken to heart. *Little fly, Thy Summer play, My thoughtless hand, Has brush'd away.* My mother's house was a spiderarium. She put tiny bug and beetle books in our Christmas stockings. The only thing I will flatten without a qualm is a mosquito – because that's a him-or-me scenario. I'd been brought up in an 'if you kill it, you have to eat it' kind of a way. Which meant that in my zealous twenties, in Ireland, when the dog killed a rabbit I followed John Seymour's *Complete Book of Self-Sufficiency* step by step. I paunched it (removed its guts), cut off its four paws, pulled its skin and fur away from its flesh (I can still hear the tear), cut off its tail, skinned it, cut off its head, stewed it up and ate it. The body, not the head, that is. Seymour says a real countryman will paunch a rabbit with its own sharp claw.

We didn't get a gun. Yet all year round the killing went on, from constant mishap to outright murder. It started small. Aphids. But whole cities of them. I patrolled the garden, my fingers flattening their plump, sap-fed bodies as easily as bursting blackcurrant skins. I squished hundreds of them. Thousands. Green juice ran down my hands and now I knew what was really meant by *green fingers*. Where were my morals now? I was being ordained. It was on one of these aphid raids in the broad-bean patch that I noticed an ant carrying an aphid up a bean stem and depositing it, alive, on the growing tip. And then another. I liked watching ants. Purposeful. Intent. Caviar on legs. Put your finger in front of an ant and quick as lightning it will choose another route. It can rear up like a stallion. And its antennae move expressively, just like in a cartoon. I admired them. I didn't suspect I'd ever have to do away with them. Until I learnt that the transportation of the aphids was the ants' farming technique to create sugary feeding zones for themselves. As the aphids sucked the sap, so the ants sucked their sugary secretions. Soon the broad beans stopped growing. Each morning my fingers got greener, but the more aphids I squashed, the faster the ants replaced them. The ants had to go. I knew where various nests were. But I was done with poison. The best method, I decided, would be quick and brutal. I boiled the kettle. Sensitive reader, turn away your eye, skip to the next paragraph. The nest I selected to exterminate was under a strip of black polythene put down to act as a barrier to keep the weeds out. I exposed the tell-tale funnel hole of the ants' nest and the small hump of fine tilth swarming with soldiers coming and going. I apologised then poured and grimaced as the steam geysered out. Surviving ants at the perimeter tore about the disaster zone collecting their large pale eggs. And then I heard a bashing sound. A sort of slapping against the black polythene. I followed the sound, bash, bash. I unfolded the curled-over polythene. A frog. Oh Jeremy, your lovely long legs, my handsome friend. The steaming water had spilled into a tube in the polythene and collected at the end where the frog was hiding. It made two more vain leaps, its powerful thigh muscles fully extended, its pale lemony belly with the veins showing through, then slumped back into the water that had been its doom. I had boiled a frog. I stared in sick disbelief. I couldn't garden all day. I buried the frog in the raspberries.

So I read up about companion planting. Plant marigolds (*Tagetes*) and nasturtiums (*Tropaeolum majus*) to ward off pests. Pests, the kind of word designed to make you spit it out. To ward off pests? But the nasturtiums were clambering all over the purple sprouting broccoli and they were *infested* with cabbage white caterpillars, and there were so many whitefly on the beech hedge that if I opened my mouth anywhere nearby they flew in. Marigolds attract hoverflies which predate on aphids. I can buy hoverflies apparently. But how many would I need? And what if I were away when these pest-eating bugs were delivered? They might starve on the doorstep. So instead I ordered some nematodes to eat the slugs, which you mix up with water then pour into the soil. The slugs survived, but the peas died of a nematode infection in the roots and the slugs kept on coming. Small pink pearly ones. Fat black leathery ones, five inches long. The snails I launched gently over the footpath because the whorl of their shells seduced me, but there was no reprieve for slugs. Slugs were collected, their tacky cold bonelessness, their wet weight tickling in my hand, then dispatched. The killing methods varied. Sometimes I stamped on them with a *sorry* and a yell – not a gleeful yell, a *yugh* yell, vicious but quick. Sometimes I put salt on them and watched them flay out like a dressed radish, then turn inside out and dissolve (I quickly stopped doing that), sometimes I drowned them – which is not a good way either, they die slowly in a floating ballet limbo, twirling around like chiffon, into a slow percolation of slug broth. Which stinks. Now and again I acted in the manner of a power-crazed despot, and a lucky slug, or a particularly large or beautiful one, would be spared and go flying on the summer's breeze with the snails into the next-door field. Maybe it was one of these slugs which climbed into our car and dried out, slowly, on the passenger-side floor. I mused over the slim coal-black coral stalactite, thinking it possibly part of an earring dropped by a friend. Until I put my glasses on and saw the exquisite markings, the tell-tale saddle, the chain-mail armour, etched by a miniaturist, its little frill skirt. A perfect slug. Desiccated. Straight. Hard. Beautiful. With a point at one end. I kept it amongst the treasures on the windowsill, with the flint scrapers, meteorites, stone eggs, pipe heads, china chips and teacup handles. I showed it to Ned, my neighbour's seven-year-old son.

'Guess what it is?' I challenged him. I held open my hand, but didn't let him touch.

He looked. 'Don't know.'

'Go on. Look closer. I'm not telling you.'

'What is it?' he said.

I put it in his small boy's hand. 'Careful,' I warned.

He looked again, holding it very carefully, then looked up and shrugged.

'Look!' I said again, he was getting fed up. 'It's . . . a . . . SLUG!'

He peered down, his nose almost touching it. A hushed boy's awe.

'See,' I pointed out the scallops on its rock-hard armour.

'It's dead,' he said.

'Yes,' I said. 'Very.'

Ned became transfixed by the desiccated slug and kept visiting it. I told him it belonged to a class of creatures called *gastropods*, meaning 'bellyfoot'. We agreed it was a good name. I suggested a little herd of bellyfoots spaced tastefully along a leather thong would make a lovely necklace. For Mum. Well, unless it were to rain. Would they rehydrate, we wondered, and his eyes popped out. The slug bewitched him and he couldn't leave it alone. Until the day . . .

'It broke,' Ned said, white-faced, holding half a snapped slug in each hand.

'Oh, no! How did it break?' I asked, mortification all over my face.

Then he began to cry.

He was only testing it, he said. To see if it would break. Now he was going to make me another. I wasn't sure how I felt about this. I fetched the barn owl pellets I'd been saving, which we could break together, to see what was inside. Mouse claws, voles' teeth, matted fur – I tempted him – bouquets of ribcages, scap-ulas and femurs as thin as dried grass. We broke open each dark baked loaf to reveal the detritus of murder. Then, like Mary Shelley, we played God with what we found and made another creature entirely.

Murder. Unwittingly and wittingly I had joined in. Slugs, aphids, whitefly, mealy cabbage fly, bean weevil, sucking things, scabs and chewing things, things that bit perfect semi circles, things that turned leaves into lace. I brewed up tobacco wash and garlic spray, stewed green potato skins, rhubarb leaves; I draped rank-smelling elder over fruit trees. I was stamping, drowning, squishing, kill-kill-killing all day.

But not moles. Too furry. Too warm-blooded. Too blind. Too difficult. Then a molehill appeared in the dining room. Were we the only people in Britain to have a molehill in their dining room? A pile of chalky earth and flints and stones had been pushed up through the brick floor (laid straight on the chalk) beside the dogs' bed. A whole bucketful. I shovelled it out, swept it up and chucked it onto the flower bed. I put badger shit down the run. The next morning – the same amount of soil again. I wheeled a barrow to the back door and shovelled the earth out. The mole had crossed the line. But I didn't know what to do. I tried filling the tunnel, but every few days, there it would be again – a molehill in the dining room. Jonathan bought a humane trap. The mole avoided it. Then Jonathan bought a normal trap. I am relieved to report that that didn't catch him either (we couldn't use it), and eventually the mole went away.

But the garden was under attack from every angle, from the

wasps in the apples to the blackbirds eating the soft fruit; a blazing bullfinch tore off all the apple blossom like Caligula at a Dionysian orgy, while pigeons (rather eatable-looking themselves) stripped the broccoli. Scarers were vetoed for aesthetic reasons – we didn't want CDs hanging in the garden, or tin foil or, God forbid, plastic bottles. Instead we jigsawed a couple of sharp-beaked terror-parrots out of marine ply and strung them up on bits of wire. The wire sagged and the stiff parrot-raptors bobbed jerkily, one wing curled up in the sun, the other down. Then the beans climbed all over them, and when I turned round forgetting they were dangling behind me, one almost pecked out my eye.

When it wasn't all death, it was obsession. I flicked through the gardening books, but learnt not to believe them. Monty, you just *can't* trim the hedge, dig, double dig, mulch, mow the lawn, prune the roses, prune the fruit trees, spray with copper, tie back, support, cut down, raise the beds, blowtorch the weeds in the brick paths, sow seeds, prick out, plant out, mulch again, add plenty of compost, mow the compost(!), take hardwood cuttings, take softwood cuttings, take leaf cuttings, have a plastic bag ready in your pocket, collect seeds, remove all infected leaves, shell peas, pick raspberries, lift dahlias, separate, divide, replant, manure, dead-head, weed, burn all infected parts!

You just can't. You'd need an army. And these are just jobs that *need to be done*, apparently. Weed. As far as weeds are concerned, the word *weedy* should mean strong, rampant, fecund. When do we ever get to *sit* in the garden? There is no loitering here. No daydreaming ferment. No counting bloody foxglove freckles.

Gardening is counter-Darwinian. It is the enabling of the

survival of the weakest. It is against Nature. It is months of travail for a blossom that might last a day. No, there is no lazing in the garden, but on a clear night when the winterbourne stream is a thin moon thread, I can sit on the swing, lean right back and stare into the blue-black velvet and think of spiral galaxies, and pulsars, and red giants, and oort clouds, and try to picture the largest volcano on Mars, which is called Olympus Mons (bad name), which is 370 miles across the base, and sixteen miles above the surrounding terrain.

I don't know how one can garden without getting blood on one's hands. Red blood, green blood, cold blood, hot blood. And tragic blood. A baby hedgehog died tangled up in the soft fruit netting. A terrified young fox cub, the bottom of his jaw shot off by the gamekeeper, came to hide behind our garden shed where he died of starvation. A faun on the footpath had its back broken by a pet lurcher and its mother wouldn't leave it. When the wildlife rescue man came, it died from a heart attack in his arms in the ensuing terror of being taken away from its mother. The man wasn't taking it to the vet to mend it, but because he said it had to be put down. He refused to leave the dead faun for the mother, but took it away to cremate. Our 'humane' madnesses. The mother remained at the spot for three days. Crazed and confused and waiting.

Our bird table was also the sparrowhawk's bird table. And with two dogs there was rabbit death (with screaming) on a regular basis. The dogs didn't seem to bite their prey, it just fell dead in their mouths, or not – I can still see the oceanic stare of the pheasant looking at me as they chewed upon its wing.

After more than a decade I have and have not become hardened to life and death in the garden. I know that, like the books about it, the garden is a place of deception. That green beans hide. That one mouse can dig up every pea that you plant, and every snowdrop bulb. That slug supply is endless. That Nature is one up on you. The garden is an Old Testament kind of a place, in all its gory glory. There will always be disaster, a baby grass snake will drown in the pond, a blue tit will fly into the window, a sparrowhawk will set its sights on your favourite dove. I march in front of Jonathan with his (rationed) strimmer, prodding at the long grass with a stick to herd any frogs or mice or slowworms out of the way. I've learnt that to interfere less is the most effective way of killing less. Arbours, espaliered avenues, foxtail lilies and herb knots are yesterday's dream. The poisonous days of 'lawn-grooming' are over. Flowers that bloom for a week or a fortnight have to look after themselves. The dynamic spectacle of the action-packed critter world is the focus of our garden now. Places they can nest. Things they can eat. What could be more joyous than seeing a cloud of long-tail tit babies landing in the elder on their first fledge? Or the blossomiest living blossom of the fiery red bullfinch bobbing around in the apple tree – he is welcome, we will have enough apples. Feather blossoms can last all year, and are less work than flowerbeds.

But then, on a summer's day, go round a table holding the very first sweet pea bloom of the year and tell your friends to sniff, and watch their shoulders drop, their heads tilt back, and swoon . . . They want more. I have it. Elusive. Beguiling.

Painted Lady, sweet pea, see *Lathyrus Odoratus.*

THE BAD MATCHMAKER

I could hardly contain myself once I'd thought of it. It was *so* perfect. It was meant to be. Roland. Yes, my friend, Roland, an artist who made curious films of snakeskin cowboy boots walking down suburban Croydon streets, with names like *Shooters Row*, who put soundtracks to films of starlings flying from power lines as if taking off from a musical score; Roland, funny, articulate, off-beat, deep-voiced; Roland, whom all the girls had secretly fallen for at one time or another; Roland, whose ideas charged out in a runaway stampede, who read Pepys in bed, whose note-book was hippopotamus fat and as promising as a birthing sow, who *always* left everything behind, and who, yes, *Oh yes!*, who spoke Spanish.

And Conchita. Of course. *Con chi-chi-chi-chita.* Mexican Chita. Whom I'd met dancing on a large flat roof in Barcelona so many years ago. Whose 500-kilowatt smile shot out across the warm summer night's terrace brighter than all the swags of fairy lights strung across it. I thought maybe she was stoned, but she was just one of those warm-hearted people who can just let go. Her blue-black hair knotted in a loose fist down her back swinging as she danced and danced and danced.

Of course. Roland, and Chita.

In our last few months of living in Barcelona, before we moved to London, Jonathan and I saw a lot of Chita. She was in the process of breaking up with her Italian husband, whom she'd married when she was eighteen. She was exuberant and dazzling, her creativity all in its raw state – romantic, unleashed, the energy flicking out in sparks. We'd kept in touch, off and on, over the years. The last time I saw her she told me to find her a man. She went for silent brooding types or spiritual gurus who meditated all day, or artists with self-obsessions and quick tempers, or writers with short moments of fleeting genius and long moments of self-doubt. All the nice men had been taken, she told me. Her email address said it all: *FloraFuego@*. . . Yes, Mexican Chita, spontaneous Chita, yes, yes. Roland and Chita couldn't be better matched. *Hmmm,* I hummed knowingly.

'Er, ye-es . . .' agreed my agreeable husband. 'Unless . . .'

'Unless what?'

Jonathan's brow knitted. 'You don't think they might both be a bit . . . disaster-prone?'

A doubt flew in, then straight out again. 'So? They will understand each other. And Chita would be sweet with Robinson,' I clucked. 'They could visit each other and have a wonderful long-distance *other* life.'

Robinson was Roland's son. He was fifteen. He could not talk but he had his own language. He had long beautiful hands and a long beautiful face. Robinson needed full-time care, so when

Roland wasn't working he was looking after Robinson. When he wasn't looking after Robinson, he was working. Which meant that Roland had very little downtime for himself. Which was why, I thought, he needed it.

I pulled out the postcard Conchita had recently sent. A black-and-white interior of a large empty old stone house over which she had superimposed a strange Lorca-esque stage-set in blood-red nail varnish and glued-on petals. *PHANTOMS OF LIFE IN THE EMPTY HOUSE*, she'd written. Across the two cultures and the two languages, it was hard to gauge how much was lost (and gained) in the translation, but her missives always made me grin. Her English was so extravagant, so Chita. The drawing or collage or poem or whatever it was would have been dashed off spontaneously, in seconds.

How good to stop, near the border. Everything is in itself, without a significance, as myself. How good to feel the changes it provokes in a day and a night and a day and a night. Not belonging to any incumstance. No memories. No future. No anguish. No man yet! Not even a *clin d'oeil* with a man. I dream to let free my wish. A sign, a whisper, someone who spends his time in writing, a voice through the telephone, in the distance, not so far now? A brief contact to tell you, Feliz Año Nuevo! START WITH GOOD FOOT. I am changing address. I wish I could change the skin. Who knows. Sometimes things that you wish come true! (what a danger).

    Chita

The grand plan took hold in my head when I discovered that from Bournemouth, forty minutes from our home, you could fly direct to Valencia, where Chita now lived. I emailed her to suggest a visit. The reply came swiftly.

It's hyper great to hear of you and I'd like very very much to see you. Hummm. Did I tell you that I am studying cultural project design? I continue my tries with a lot of determination to find a way of living that adds some pepper and joy. I really would like to visit you, your dogs, your garden and your eating. Just tell me when. You are like an angel right now. I wait for your answer and to look at possibilities.

    Love, Chita

I was straight on the phone to Roland. I knew in the summer
he had every other weekend free, but I didn't know which. But
I did know I had to pin him down. But I didn't want to frighten
him off. I told him I had a friend I really wanted him to meet.
Hey, I've got a friend coming to stay I really want you to meet. But I
didn't make too much of it. We settled on the last weekend in
June. Perfect. Then I remembered that Roland, being so time-
poor, could be a little unreliable, so I told him, serious-joking,
that it was written in blood. Immediately I heard a hesitation,
but ignored it, telling myself he was accustomed to me overstating
things. I dashed off an email to Chita with the dates. A day later,
two emails arrived in my inbox: Chita, and Roland. Well, there's
a good sign.

Great, great, great! In this stage of my life to feel welcome
is the best of gifts I can dream of. Thank you so much. I
was waiting for an inspiring destination for the last week of
June and now I have it. I confirm timetables: Flight FR9911
arrive BOH at 14.00. Some days before let me know about
weather to select my clothes (something elegant, just in
case?) Looking forward to seeing you in your own territory.
Kissessss.

Chita

Who is this person you want me to meet? I'd love to see
you two too . . . so I'll write in sweat rather than blood.
Love to your animals, vegetables and selves,

Roland

Hi Roland

    A Mexican friend living in Spain is coming to stay for a few days ... and you speak Spanish ... How about weekend 25/26 etched in sweat, but hopefully no tears?

    K x

Damn. He was bound to smell a rat. I told Chita to bring boots.

    – Boots! I look forward to beautiful walks. Any special need from Spain? How much wine can I bring? Are you inviting a lot of male candidates to your party? ChuChuChu The Mexican lady ready for new adventures ... God bless you.

    Chita

Ola Chita

    As far as male candidates, remember quality not quantity! Nearer the time I will let you know what the weather is doing.

    K x

I liked *Ola* Chita, it also means *wave* Chita.

'It's all going a bit *too* smoothly,' I told Jonathan.

'What do you mean?'

'He's going to cry off. I just know it.'

I imparted my plan to Judy, who was a mutual friend of Roland's. I showed her a photograph of Chita. My excitement was infectious. We agreed Roland must not bottle out. We agreed there was every chance he would. Another postcard arrived. A flower unfurling with a collage of flames licking out.

Inmovile in the middle of the forest, feeling the scent of the air, listening the drops over the dry leafs and the vibrations of life under my feet. Contemplating. This is not a poem. Just impressions. They disappear very fast. They seem not to exist and yet they can stop the time and make me feel alive. What to do?

Chita

My agreeable husband looked glum as I walked in the door. 'He's cancelled,' he said.

'What?'

'I got a text.' Jonathan shook his head, knowing that I would be crestfallen.

'Why?'

'He's in Wales. Working on a composition.'

'But he promised! I knew it! Fuck. Fuck. Fuck.'

I was straight on the phone to Judy. 'He's cancelled.'

'No!'

'Can you believe it?'

'Oh no.'

'I *knew* this would happen.'

'Oh dear.'

'This could have been a lovely thing in his life. Someone to escape to every now and again. And a lovely thing in her life too. It would have been so perfect.'

'I'll ring Cait,' Judy said. 'She'll talk to him.'

It was true. Cait was Roland's best friend and probably the only person who might persuade him. She could say anything to

him, she'd known him for years. She'd seen him through thick
and thin, but mostly thin.

That evening, an email from Roland in my inbox:

I could come Sunday, but probably wouldn't arrive till eleven
a.m., but I can stay over Sunday eve. Let me know.
Roland

Great! Let Sunday be etched on your bones.
Kx

One night with a day either side would have to be enough. I
felt like a bully, though, gobbling up every moment of Roland's
precious time, and I wished I'd been able to engineer it without
such brute force. On 24 June, I set off to pick up Conchita.

I saw her the moment I drove up, standing outside Arrivals.
Her flight must have come in early. She looked worried, but her
face lit up when she finally saw me. We hugged. She squeezed
me so hard my sunglasses stuck into my face. I bundled her bags
in the car and we drove away.

It took less than ten minutes for a deep sinking feeling to settle.
I was silent as Chita regaled me with details of her inner states.
Words like *fire*, *flight*, *heart*, *soul*, *desire*, *destiny* and *pain* rushed out.
I could feel my face freeze into a pained smile. She said I was an
angel, but her mouth was turned downwards as she spoke, her
eyebrows knitted into deep furrows. This was a worrying start. Had
I not been aware of the extent of the inner turmoil of this passionate
soul? Or had I just forgotten? The last few occasions we met, brief

as they were – a dinner, a swim, a snatched lunch – she had, now I came to think about it, been on a sort of helter-skelter of elation, to descend only moments later into torment and anguish. At the time, I'd put this down to the upset of her life and Latin fire. And I have always been attracted to free spirits and a bit of untamed wildness. Fine for me, but not so fine for Roland, or for Chita, for that matter. But now I was thinking about it more carefully, something buried was resurfacing – that maybe there *was* a glimmer of a suspicion that a darker force was at work here. The Chita sitting next to me now was a troubled Chita, on the edge of a precipice. At any moment she could be soaring up to heady heights or plummeting down into the abyss. If I knew anything at all, I knew this was one thing Roland could definitely do without.

The first evening of Chita's stay we were invited to a neighbour's birthday celebration. We had to walk across two fields. Chita looked breathtaking. Head-turningly divine in night-sky velvet and a rose silk shawl. She sang all the way there and spent the evening charming the hosts, then playing with their children upstairs. I looked across the crowd a couple of times and saw her laughing with some lucky guests toasting themselves in the warmth she radiated. What had I been worrying about? This was the Chita I remembered. But the following day my fear was rekindled. I found poems written on tree bark. Jonathan's boyhood eyeless teddy, who lived in the spare room, had been put downstairs (and chewed by the dogs), because, she said, the bear had been staring at her. Foolishly, we watched a DVD of the Frida Kahlo movie, *Frida*. Chita identified wholly as Kahlo in whom she found a connection to her deepest psyche. Tears filled her eyes. Anything – and, it seemed, almost everything – reminded her of her own life's disappointments, of things she'd lost, and of what was lacking. I worried about her. There seemed nothing I could say that did not double back onto her situation. Everything was profound and intense. Everything I tried to make things better only seemed to make them worse. Far worse. I became wooden, tongue-tied, drained, nervous, allergic.

'Do you read much, Chita?' I asked, as we drove to the shop to buy some milk.

'Well, I have nothing in my life,' her smile folded downwards. 'No person to take my time, or love in any way, so of course I have much time for reading books,' she said.

I began to treat her like an invalid. Rugs, hot water bottles. She began to get ill. I changed tack. We made bread together. I said kneading bread was wonderful because you could take out all your frustration on the dough. Like a punch bag. She began to knead. Punching and punching. Then her shoulders sagged. She broke down in floods of tears and told me her last lover was arrested for beating her.

'But I thought he was some kind of meditating holy guy?'

'So much hatred. How could someone hate me so much to want to kill me?'

'Oh, Chita,' I said. 'You don't want to be with someone like that.'

'I made him something beautiful for his birthday. He wrote to me with terrible hate. How can someone say such bad things when you have made something with so much love?'

'Meditators are a worry,' I said. 'They're always, well, meditating. One is dead, surely, long enough.'

She looked nonplussed.

'Chita, I think it might help to dampen the fire. Just a little. Of course your fire is beautiful, but sometimes it is raging out of control. Maybe you need to earth yourself.'

She was staring at me. I thought I was getting somewhere. I continued, emboldened. We could try together? Put the fire aside, just for a while. Little things, I suggested. Her email address for example, maybe it was too . . . inflammatory? I told her that although I loved it, I could also see it as metaphorically shoring up a passionate image that might be too intoxicating. Whereas something like, say . . . FloraRio, might be more calming? I was heading down a rabbit hole fooling myself I was climbing a mountain. I said I thought she was flying too high and diving too low and that it might damage her. She watched my hand movements. She told me other people had talked to her this way and used the same hand movements. I said that the world, that people, might not be able to live up to such high hopes and expectations. Her face fell. Her beautiful eyes were drooping like a deer's. I was in too deep. I knew I must back off. Because I knew I could not see it through.

On Sunday morning, Roland arrived at eleven. It was the hottest day of the year. Spanish hot, even. We lazed around in the garden. Chita followed me into the kitchen to tell me that I was right about Roland. I smiled and gulped. Outside I could see my agreeable husband rattling a large plastic zip-up bag. Roland grinned.

Oh no. Oh please no.

Jonathan and Roland had taken advantage of the final two weeks when you could legally buy fresh Mexican magic mushrooms online before new legislation came in. They'd bought half a kilo between them and Jonathan had been drying them in the garage. As far as he and Roland were concerned it couldn't be a better day.

'But we've got Bea and Roy coming for supper,' I implored.

'So? It's only eleven o'clock.'

'But you haven't tried these before. You haven't a clue what they're like.'

'Perfect opportunity. Isn't it, Roland?'

I wanted to rein this in, but didn't want to look like I was reining it in. I didn't want to be the *controlling* person. But this was definitely not in my plans. This was insider sabotage.

'What about Chita?' I looked across, willing her to veto it.

'I don't know,' she said. 'I have never tried these things. Are they fun?'

'*Very* fun,' laughed Roland. 'We hope!'

'Come on, it's Roland's day off.' Jonathan said. 'It will be fine.'

'Really?' I sounded unconvinced. 'Well, it's up to everyone else,' I said curmudgeonly.

Roland took three. Jonathan five! I took one. Chita took one.

'Take a half,' I said.

'Why?'

'Well, I don't know, maybe . . .'

'But if I take a half and you all take more, then . . .' She lifted her shoulders, eyes wide and round.

'If you're sure, Chita.'

'Well, I am *not* sure.'

Nor was I. Except about one thing. I was furious with Jonathan. I breathed out loudly and stared hard at my disagreeable husband with his fistful of shrivelled-limbed homunculi, but he swallowed them all. Blue ones, brown ones.

I've never really been a drug-taker, not even in my very early youth. If I ever smoked anything it was more, as a reformed smoker, for the tobacco. But I had quite liked the zaniness of mushrooms. There was something *natural* about them. Organic. I liked stories of indigenous peoples dancing for three days. Or the Laplanders who discovered the hallucinogenic properties of amanita as they watched their reindeer get hooked on the fungus and leap gigantically about. In Ireland I took magic mushrooms a few times in my twenties and once laughed for two days. How glorious to laugh for two days. In Mexico I washed down the tongue-drying peyote cactus with coconut milk still in its shell, followed by shots of tequila, and swam the whole night under the stars in a warm phosphorescent sea. I wasn't so bothered about the drugs, but I did like the freedom and I did like laughing. Whenever I saw schoolgirls on the train in hysterical laughter, I smiled. I knew how it felt, well, happy, intoxicating, exhausting. So maybe this would be all right? Then maybe it was just what we needed. Maybe it was just what Conchita needed. Laughter. The best medicine. So I went with it. I popped my mushroom in my mouth. Then immediately began to worry again. But then I thought we could have a really nice time, and let all the intensity just float away, and everyone could get on really well. And then I thought, maybe too well. Conchita might become smitten with Roland. And if anything was crystal clear to me by now it was that my matchmaking plans for Roland were a really bad idea. Just the last straw of complication he did not need. And it would be the last thing Chita needed too. And it would all be my doing. She could fall head over heels, and Roland, in some stoned, thick-hided, male way, could be oblivious to everything. He was so friendly, he might unwittingly lead her on. And she was so friendly and beautiful and . . . By now I was chewing my cheek. I swore to God I would *never* bloody matchmake again; no, from now on, I would *never, ever* meddle in other people's lives.

Absolutely nothing. Zilch. Not a thing. We were gardening. Planting seedlings in the vegetable patch. I looked across to Chita. Hadn't seen her happier. It was sunny and calm. She was trilling away, humming and laughing a bit.

'Are you okay, Chita?'

'Yes. I feel nothing.'

But barely a few seconds later, I had to admit to myself I was beginning to feel a bit nauseous. And then I was beginning to feel a *lot* nauseous.

Jonathan and Roland were lying on the lawn with the dogs, talking about building coracles and swimming in streams. We went and joined them. The conversation got more and more divergent and winding and outlandish, then more tangential and a bit surreal. Chita rolled over, stroked a dog. I could see that Roland and Jonathan were really quite out of it. They talked. On and on. I joined in. Then I started to laugh. My head hurt. We were all laughing. Except Chita was lying facing the other way. She was hugging the dog. I could see her shoulders begin to shake. Up and down. Was she laughing too? I hadn't a clue but I suspected the worst. And then she ran away.

I caught up with her in the kitchen. She turned. Her mouth strung like a bow, the stricken face of tragedy.

'Chita? Chita?'

'Oh, I am so isolated,' she wailed.

'What do you mean, isolated? We're all together.'

'I don't understand. I don't understand what's happening.'

'We're a bit out of it, that's all. We're being a bit stupid.'

'Stupid? What do you mean stupid?'

'I mean silly. *Tonta. Tontaria. Estupida.* You know, messing about, joking, ridiculous, a bit stoned.'

'But this is not stoned.'

'Well, no, it's . . . it's sort of like that, though.'

'But I don't understand what you are saying. I don't know what you are talking about. I don't know your lives. I don't know you. You all have each other. I never have friends like this. How do you have friends like this? In Spain it is not so. I am alone. Alone.' A sob shuddered out of her.

My nausea was really setting in. The sun streamed in the window. I could see Jonathan and Roland lying in the sun, talking, laughing. Oblivious – of course. I felt an overwhelming urge to back out of the kitchen, to just go and lie in the sun.

'Chita, come back. Be with us. It's all right. It's just the mushrooms making you feel paranoid. It will pass. I promise you. I'm sorry. We should never have taken them. It's all my fault, I should never have let them.'

'No, but you cannot be sorry. I *have* taken them. I am old enough. I have made the decision.'

'Yes, but if you've never taken them before, well, it wasn't a good idea. It was stupid of us. Completely stupid.'

'No, but now I spoil everything. I have ruined everything. How can I go back now? This experience is giving evidence to me who I am. Who I cannot be. I came in hope of a miracle. All the open windows in my head are shouting, *Who are you?*'

I stood there, not knowing what to say. Conchita with such high hopes of a rescue mission. And it could not be going more horribly wrong.

'It is a terrible feeling. A terrible feeling,' she cried.

'I know I . . .' I *really* wanted to lie in the sun, really, really a lot.

'When will it stop? When will it stop?'

'It will stop. I don't know when exactly. But very soon. You will feel better. I promise. This is just the bad bit.'

'Bad bit? You never told me about a bad bit.'

'I didn't know. I'm sorry. I . . .'

I tried to tell her about the Laplanders and the reindeer.

'I must leave tomorrow. I shouldn't have come and brought my problems with me.' She looked at me suspiciously. The look got worse.

Terrific. Here in front of me was the one person who should *never* try mushrooms. I had managed to drag her out of her country and set up a situation to tip her over the edge. With a bit of self-doubt, self-loathing and humiliation thrown in. Well done. Very much the ex-angel now.

Outside the sun was shining, the ash tree leaves were fluttering, Jonathan and Roland were still laughing, lying on the grass, still oblivious to the meltdown.

'Oh but Chita, we were having such a nice day, it's lovely outside, let's go and lie under the tree. Please, let's all be together.'

My head was being squeezed dry. My mouth was desiccating. Drink water. Drink water. I filled up a big jug. How could my first attempt at matchmaking go so wrong? Then I remembered who, in the first place, led us all astray.

'We have to ride this bit out,' I told Chita, 'it will pass.'

I gave her a glass of water.

'Let's eat something,' I said.

I reeled over towards the bread bin and started hacking off slices of bread. Then I made a salad with rice and things I found in the fridge. The effort was gargantuan. My head wanted to go horizontal and my eyes wanted to watch clouds. Shit, it was nearly two o'clock. And I had to get dinner sorted. Then Chita ran off.

Roland and Jonathan were still lying on the grass laughing.

'Guys, you've got to help. She's spinning out. She's never taken them before.'

'Oh no.' They both looked genuinely concerned. 'Bring her back.'

'She's embarrassed. She feels left out.'

'Bring her back. We should all be together.'

I found Chita in the bathroom and persuaded her to come out. She leant heavily on me as we made our way across the lawn. The dogs accompanied us. She bent down to stroke Jessie.

Roland and Jonathan gave her a big hug. They apologised and told her it would be all right.

'You like it?' she asked.

'Yes,' they smirked, they did.

'But I feel like I'm falling,' she said. 'Like the sky is charging away.'

They liked that, they said. She seemed to calm down. Then without warning she was up again, running across the lawn out of the gate and across the field. Even the dogs looked spooked. They followed. I followed. We all followed. Chita was making a strange winnowing noise. She was dancing, then she crumpled on her knees again.

'When will it stop?'

'When *will it* stop?' I asked Roland and Jonathan. I felt shit, too. I assumed much of it was the exhaustion of trying to hold it all together, of swimming against the tide and trying not to say the wrong thing for three days – and what made it even worse was that Jonathan and Roland still looked like they were having a really nice time.

'Big error,' I muttered to my agreeable husband, under my breath.

'It'll be fine. It'll be fine.'

'For you, maybe. And what about supper?' I glared.

Now Chita was standing out in the field in the long meadow grass between two ash trees. Her arms were outstretched and her head was dangling like a crucifixion. Her face was contorted. I was hoping our neighbour wouldn't come past. Then the crucifixion turned into a dance. The dogs were not sure what to do. Jump up or leave well alone. They left well alone.

Half an hour later we were all lying on the lawn again. Conchita was curled up in the foetal position with Jonathan stroking her back. She began to cry. He told her everything was all right. Roland stroked her back too. She cried some more. They hugged her. They rocked her shoulder gently like a baby in a cradle. Her crying got less and less. Then started up again, and got more and more. Roland said mushrooms can open all sorts of doors. (Including some best left shut, I feared.) He said lots of other comforting things. Roland and Jonathan are naturally kind, that is their nature. Their kindness began to mortify Chita. She said she had spoilt our day. I was thinking this whole matchmaking malarkey had spoilt the week.

An hour later and everything was happy. Chita was dancing to Cuban music in the house. I was in a hammock. The boys were in the same place they started in. Slowly everything started to ease out. We walked down to the river to a small swimming hole and jumped in. We swam in circles, round and round. The water was cool and clear. And everything was okay. We had dinner outside, candles flickering, some miracle salad and a chicken that appeared to have roasted itself. Our guests were none the wiser. The remaining mushrooms were buried (by me) deep in the compost heap.

A few weeks later a bulging letter arrived from Spain. I tore open the envelope, and it was full of red leaves. Chita wrote that she had recaptured her sense of herself.

But my real identity is like a feather that I try to capture in a windy day. I need to be light and transparent as an angel but I don't know how to do it. Maybe I should concentrate on the words which were said at the mass from the Apocalypse: 'There was a woman with a dress of sun, standing on the moon with a crown made of twelve beams of diamonds'.

'That was bad of us,' I said to Jonathan. 'I feel bad, I wish I was a better person.'

'Easy in hindsight. I'm not sure what we could have done?'

'I could have stopped you. Thrown away those bloody mushrooms.' Blame subtly transferred to him.

'No you couldn't,' Jonathan said.

We talked around it for days, but we both knew we should have been more responsible, that we shouldn't have let it happen. We had not been our best selves. I sent Chita a book of Mimmo Paladino prints. There were pictures of hands reaching out, and faces, goblets and night birds, with a sense of both dizziness and equilibrium. Chita was a woman with a dress of sun standing on the moon with a crown made of twelve beams of diamonds. We were children of the earth and its dark deeds.

THE ANTICIPATED CELEBRATION

What we once called The Birthday Weekend, we now call The Birthday Debacle. It wasn't the weather, even though we left London at the end of April in a balmy 26° C, and got off the overnight sleeper (first class) at Pitlochry Station in sub-zero wind-lashing rain. And it wasn't the train, even though our eagerly anticipated dinner of haggis and neeps came out of a tin. We loved it anyway. We were excited; I told the guard we were excited. We struck up conversation with a retired nuclear physicist and his wife going to Skye. Where else could you do that, but on a train to Scotland? It felt like an adventure, as if we'd gone back in time. The problem was the hotel.

Jonathan found it. It wasn't the B&B on Rannoch Moor I had set my heart on, because when Jonathan rang months and months ago, the owner told him not to worry, he could book nearer the time, and so instead of booking there and then, he rang back nearer the time when it was fully booked. So this was the replacement hotel. A fifteenth-century coaching inn on a loch! Alastair Sawday's guidebook recommended it. And it had been awarded

Good Hotel Guide 2007 Inn of the Year. 'It's your birthday,' Jonathan said, 'we can't stay in a B&B'. For this wasn't any birthday, it was a landmark birthday with a nought at the end.

'And it has a library,' he said.

'A library?' I repeated, with wistful longing.

And here's the odd thing: I had never really stayed in a hotel before. Not in Britain anyway, not a proper one. There had been no occasion for me to do so. In far-flung places I had stayed in pensions and cheap hotels, or bamboo huts on the beach, but nearer home it was always B&Bs, or friends, or camping.

I imagined peat fires, and long walks, and kippers for breakfast, and whisky in heavy glasses. So I got him to check. *Yes, yes, peat fires, kippers for breakfast.* They told him they had a room where you could see the loch from the bath. He booked the room. I saw mullioned windows and musty antiquarian leather-bound books about lairds and Celtic battles and deer stalking. He showed me the website. It said, 'Set in ten acres of our own private gardens'. I saw rolling lawns down to cold crystal waters, and daffodils, and rhododendron bushes billowing out across the drive. It said, 'Real Scottish style hospitality'. I imagined antlers and tartan rugs and heather, and it said, 'friendly, efficient yet relaxed'. Yes, yes, we wanted relaxed. The website said, 'We will surprise you'. Yes.

It's not that the fifteenth-century Scottish coaching inn picture in my head is dashed by the prominent '70s extension with dark wood chalet-type windows. Nor the no drive, the no rhododendrons, the not many daffs, the no sweeping gardens and the no lawn to the loch. We don't care about that. The mountains will be our garden. We smile our way with our bags to reception, where the efficient South African receptionist tells us he has put us down for dinner at seven p.m. Oh, too early, we explain. He looks troubled. We suggest eight-thirty p.m. He shakes his head. Eight? Not possible, he is afraid. He has us down for seven. After quite a struggle we settle on seven-thirty. No matter, we'll probably be tired on our first night.

The South African receptionist gives us a tour of the hotel. We walk through clean lobby areas and corridors with Habitat sofas and vases of long stalks of South African dried cotton. No antlers, no mullioned windows, no tartan rugs, no heather. The library is a modern Swiss chalet with large wooden rhino ornaments, there is a wall of *magazines*, and a wall of gaudy travel books on South Africa, and a wall of cook books. The owner is also the chef, the receptionist proudly tells us. My husband used to be a chef. He worked in a well-known restaurant in Australia called You & Me. Once he cooked for the Prime Minister Bob Hawke, for his daughter's private wedding party; he has even cooked with Michel Roux! I'm hoping he doesn't get too chummy with the chef here; Jonathan is a walk in, pick up a knife and start chopping sort of a guy. The receptionist is still telling us things but I'm not listening. I just want to get to our room.

'Is it all right?' asks my apprehensive husband as we unpack our things in our squarish, tartanless, rugless, suburban-looking room.

'Yes,' I say. (That's all I say.) I squeeze his arm.

As I mentioned, we usually camp or stay in B&Bs. I've certainly never been in a hotel like this, with robes in each room and Molton Brown soap dispensers. There's no telly, which is a good thing. I don't need to watch it, and would hate the sound of other guests' tellies coming through the wall. And no radio either. That's . . . fine. We don't need Radio 4 every morning. I just hope Nelson Mandela doesn't die (he didn't, well, not for another six years). Or Bob Dylan. Those would be big historic events that I would like to know about, I feel, and I wonder how the guests felt after the Twin Towers came down and they knew nothing about it. I won't let these questions bother me, for this is The Birthday Weekend. And there is a bottle of champagne on the table and a card that reads: *Hope you have a wonderful stay, best wishes Sara and Pete.* And yes, you *can* see the loch from the bath. Until the loch disappears – but that's not the bath's fault. Until later I discover that it actually is. The mist from the hot water makes the windows fog up on the inside. But that doesn't matter because there is already mist on the outside, and then it begins to rain so you can't see the loch anyway. But I've always liked the rain. We can read. But not in bed. No sitting up in this £300 per night bed (yes, I eventually bludgeon this information out of my spoiling-me-rotten husband), because the roof slopes away at a forty-five degree angle just above your head. No matter! We have two upright chairs to sit upright in. 'The dinner better be good,' I mutter to myself. It will be. 'This is the Inn of the Year.'

The dinner is good. Ish. But first we have to move our table from the one under the speaker with the very loud easy-listening piped music. A relief to Jonathan who has, on a previous painful occasion, witnessed me pull out the wires. I have osso buco, but it was stupid of me to choose anything with asparagus, when we grow our own and can cook it freshly cut straight from the garden, as we did just before we came. Although didn't the website say 'fresh local produce' on our tables? Of course, it's too early up here for asparagus; I crunch them down and don't mention a thing. I do get a bit anxious when our wine is taken away and does not reappear. It comes back. Then is taken away again. We are being punished, I suspect, because Jonathan didn't want the *someone along in a minute* to give advice on the wine. He wanted to choose it for himself. And now I come to think of it (while waiting for the hostage wine), wasn't it a bit bloody odd to be rung up in our room, five minutes before seven-thirty p.m., to be, let's say, jogged along? And, dare I say it, don't *any* Scottish people work here? Ah yes, foolish of me, Scottish *style*. Although this doesn't explain the very large black and white photographs of *Chef as Little Boy in South Africa* all the way round the white dining room. Just as I almost sarkily say something, our host, Sara, sweeps by. She knows our names, she knows it's my birthday weekend, she has perfect skin and perfect beige hair, perfect nails that glint with a sheen, her hands are perfect, latex-glove clean, her clothes are oatmeal-coloured and matching. I thank her for the champagne she left in our room – and the personal card. She graciously accepts my thanks and backs off to the next table.

Jonathan is smirking.

'What? Did you order it?'

He tells me hotels do that. It's what you pay for. He often

travels for work. In Germany, he tells me, they leave a chocolate on the pillow.

I'm slightly crestfallen. I thought it was something special they had done because he had told them it was my birthday. He shrugs kindly.

'What about the card?' I ask. 'They do that for everyone?'

He looks a bit doubtful. 'Well. Maybe that was for your birthday.'

Jonathan gets up and goes to the loo. A French waitress dives over, picks his napkin up off his chair, folds it and puts it next to his plate. No sooner has she done so than the South African waitress swoops on it and repositions it on his chair. The South African waitress glares fiercely at the French waitress. Bloody hell. That night I check my pillow, but nothing is there.

The next morning at nine-twenty a.m. our phone rings. Are we are coming down for breakfast? Yes, we are. We double-check the five pages of hotel information in the leather binder on the side table. Breakfast is served from eight-thirty a.m. until ten. We both have a kipper. A very small kipper, quite a bit smaller than my hand. With a triangle of cold toast which is put on our table – this time away from the speaker – almost the moment we sit down. We get a thimble of marmalade. And a bottle-top of butter. But they're probably right. It's uncouth having one of those fabulously *huge* B&B breakfasts that last you all day. I suppose you might say it's more *delicate* here. The milk jug is petite. So we have to ask twice for more milk and then we have to ask for it to be heated for the very weak coffee out of the very small cafetière. Who cares. Not us. Not until we are cornered within five minutes of sitting down to breakfast by the receptionist again about what frigging time we will be eating supper. Tonight we have a choice: seven or seven-thirty.

'Oh.'

The receptionist smiles a tight, efficient smile.

'Um.'

He lingers, tilting over the table slightly.

'Do you need to know now?'

He does.

'How about eight-thirty?'

'I'm sorry. Seven or seven-thirty p.m.'

We take seven-thirty. I begin to fume. I want to drive to a pub instead, but we have already paid for bed, breakfast and dinner, and it's my birthday and we are supposed to be having a fancy restaurant meal. When we get back to our room the ghosts have been in. Every time we leave it, they come. We never catch them. They like to tie the robes up. Tight. Tourniquet them around the waist. So if you quickly want to put one on, and you are dripping wet out of the loch-view bath, you have to perform an unexpected Houdini wrestle with the belt. It catches me out every time. I reach out, grab not a robe, but a corn dolly. And why am I calling them *robes*? We have dressing-gowns at home. The ghosts tidy things up. Or just move them slightly. Slip out for a second and they slip in, whatever the time of day. They empty the tiny kettle, so each time we have to fill it up again. And they empty the petite jug of milk on the tea tray (with no biscuits), so each time we have to ring for more. But worse. Much worse. The loo roll has been tampered with. These are not chocolate-on-the-pillow ghosts, they are loo roll-tampering ghosts. The ends (plural – you get a double loo roll holder for £300 a night) have been folded back into sharp points, like arrowheads. This mortifies me. That someone does this. Because lately, we have been trying to be eco-conscious and we don't *always* flush the loo. So someone had to bend over my pee (though they probably flushed the loo first – equally mortifying) to fold the end of each loo roll up into a little point. I've never heard of such a thing. My husband has. He knows all about it. Hotel-world. The more I think about it the more appalled I become. That someone does this for a job. Worse. That someone tells someone to do it. Teaches them how, probably. And even worse than that, someone, somewhere, dreamt it up in the first place. Made it part of hotel etiquette. This place is depressing me. Jonathan thinks I'm not cut out for hotels. But it's not the ghosts. Even though now, each time we get back to our room, I obsessively check to see what they've done. I lift the bed cover. Look under the bed. 'Maybe they're still here,' I say loudly. 'Maybe they actually live in this room, with us.' The loch-view window still looks like the ghosts have put tracing paper over it. As we back out of the door, I tell them to tie up the robes and fold the loo paper into sharp points.

We walk all day. In the rain over pine stumps and boggy peat tractor-ruts. We see a white mountain hare, and high on a hillside we catch a glimpse of a huge herd of about seven hundred deer. Then we drive back quickly to have just enough time for a bath and a cup of tea. At ten minutes past seven, the raincloud lifts for a moment, a glimmering silver slither slips out of the tracing paper, a sudden glitter, a shaft of sun, and the loch suddenly appears in the loch-view window. There are swifts swooping. Swifts!

'Let's go and have a look.'

Jonathan looks at his watch.

'Come on, we haven't seen it yet. It's not far. It's my birthday,' I say.

Just as we pass below our window on the way to the loch we hear the phone ringing. And ringing. And ringing and ringing. It stops. Then rings again. Do they think we are *hiding* in the room?

'What time is it?' I ask.

'Seven-twenty-four.'

I take a perverse pleasure in the sound of the phone. We walk on to the loch. Pretending not to hurry. Jonathan walking a little fast, me trying to slow him down. At *exactly* eight minutes past seven-thirty we make eye contact with our host, Sara, at the dining room door. She bars the way. Yes, her arm actually swings out to stop our path.

She says, 'You can't go in there.'

That's what she says. That. Is. What. She. Says.

We cannot enter the dining room. She ushers us into an adjoining room.

'What time was your booking?' she asks, trying to regain her composure.

'Seven-thirty,' I say in a confrontational tone.

She glances at her watch, she knows the time. She wants to know what happened.

'Nothing,' I say.

'Did you get stuck?'

'No,' I say.

'We went for a walk to the loch,' Jonathan explains. Could have chopped his ruddy tongue out.

Well, now she has to rearrange everything because their sequence is all awry. So we must be punished. Escorted to the antechamber and made to wait. After a good twenty minutes on the naughty step we are escorted into the mirthless dining room to the wrongdoers' table, right by the door. Right next to where the battalion of waiters trip over each other and whisper in Afrikaans, about *us*.

'Eight minutes!' I squawk.

'I know.'

'Eight minutes late! Not ten minutes. Not fifteen. Not twenty. Eight!' I say, biting down on the 't'.

'I know.'

'It's my birthday!'

'I know.'

We order. And wait for the wine. A suspiciously long time. It comes, is poured, and before we realise, is whisked away again.

'What if Spanish or Italian people stay here?' I say. 'They don't eat at seven o'clock. Does it say on their website, *No Spanish or Italians please*? Does it say, *No Irish*? They're *always* late. In some cultures it's impolite to be on time.'

Our glasses dry out. I ask for the bottle to be left at the table. We wait more than eight minutes before it appears again.

'They've peed in it,' I say.

'Or filled it up with water,' Jonathan suggests.

I seriously take against the place. Things deteriorate. We deteriorate. We begin calling it The Birthday Debacle. Jonathan nicknames the South African napkin-correcting waitress, who kidnaps our wine and whom we see telling off the French waitress, Badass. It has sunk to this. I go to the loo. Badass folds my napkin. I swear next time I will tie it to the back of the chair. I choose the liqueur ice cream for dessert, even though I don't like ice cream, because, as I inform Badass, it's too early for *new season strawberries* in Scotland, it's April. She gives me a professional smile that doesn't bend. Yes, it's sunk to this.

'This is a boarding school. A boot camp,' I rant. 'That woman's not a host, she's a frustrated headmistress. One more unreasonable £300-a-night intransigence on their side and we should go. I *want* to go.'

I look at the other guests, who are cowed, quiet, and doing what they are told.

'If they harass us *one more time*, if they ring us up at two minutes to, if they order us about once more, I'm off.'

My beneficent, bileless, hates-to-rock-the-boat husband agrees. 'Really?'

'Yes.'

I'm over the moon. 'We can go?'

'Of course. This is terrible.'

I am so relieved.

We don't have to wait long. As we sit down for our breakfast rations we are told dinner will be at seven-fifteen.

'Seven-fifteen?' I repeat after him, in my cut-glass voice.

The waiter nods. We sense the strain.

'We don't have a choice?'

He tips his head. Eyebrows up.

'But that is too early. We might want to have a drink in the pub after our walk. It's still light,' I say.

'Seven-fifteen is too early,' Jonathan confirms, firmly.

'I'm afraid the only time possible,' the waiter says, tight-lipped, 'is seven-fifteen.'

We nod. Tighter-lipped. But I'm delighted. I try to butter my cold toast. We ask for two jugs of milk to be heated for our coffee. They come back, lukewarm.

I enjoy packing my bag. Snooks to them. I pump the Molton Brown Indian Cress hair conditioner into my half-empty bottle of Pantene. Take four sachets of pink grapefruit tea. I triple-check the room. Then check again. In the card, after 'Hope you have a wonderful stay', I childishly write, 'As long as you do exactly as we say!' and leave it on the bedside table for the ghosts.

'Make sure we don't pay extra for that champagne,' I brief Jonathan as we bounce our cases down the stairs. 'And try not to tell them you've cooked with Michel Roux.'

Jonathan tells our host, Sara, that we are leaving. We can see her mind buzzing round. 'It's clear you cannot accommodate us,' he says.

'We feel uncomfortable,' I add. 'You made us feel uncomfortable.'

She takes a breath. 'I'm sorry,' she says, 'but you *were* late,' in a chiding sort of a way.

'Eight minutes, Sara. Eight. Not ten. Not even fifteen. Not

twenty. Eight. Eight minutes late. That's nothing. Your website, I seem to recall, says this is a *relaxed* hotel.'

'Not when it comes to dining,' she says.

She tells us they work *very hard on the dining experience*. She says her husband cooks *all* the food. She says timing is very important. I say it is obsessive. That it spoils the *experience*. Sara tells us she thinks it was *deeply disrespectful* to go for a walk before dinner. She says it is very rude to be late.

I coldly repeat, 'Eight minutes. Eight minutes.'

I tell her it's mad. Twice. I know I say *mad* twice, but I'm not sure now whether I put an *It's* or a *You're* in front of it. She begins to explain how a kitchen works. Jonathan tells her he *knows* how a kitchen works. He has cooked in a lot better restaurants than this. He tells her he has cooked with Michel Roux. She says he should understand then. I say it's she who doesn't understand. She asks us if we would keep Gordon Ramsay waiting eight minutes. I double-take. So this is how they see themselves. And it's news to me that Gordon Ramsay is a paragon of virtue, arbitrator of good manners and politesse. I remind her it was my birthday, and not just any birthday. I tell her I wanted to see the loch, I tell her the regime in the hotel is *not* relaxed, that their ethos runs *counter* to having a nice time. Something ripples across her face. It is a brainwave. She asks if we are *always* late. Nonplussed, I say we are sometimes late. Ten minutes, maybe. Here or there.

She smiles. A very self-satisfied smile. Enough said. She nods knowingly. She's won, apparently. She's proved her point. We are the late people.

We pay. We are gone. We are excited, as if we have escaped,

broken out. As we drive past the sign saying, *Not far now to Hotel A—*! I suggest we buy a spray can and tag it with *Not far now to Jo'berg. Or Robben Island. Ha Ha.* We go to the paper shop and buy the Sunday papers, which the £300-a-night hotel beginning with 'A' on Loch Tay (south side) does not get delivered. Maybe the paper shop owners were late for dinner once too. I tot up how much the £300-a-night Best Inn of the Year must save on Sunday papers and TV licences, never mind the cost of the tellies. We go to the nice outdoor-trekking shop. I buy a better pair of waterproof trousers. We tell them about the *eight minutes.* We hire a canoe. We tell the canoe man about the *eight minutes.* We climb a Munro. At a cairn in a dense wet cloud we tell some fellow walkers about the *eight minutes.* We look for somewhere to stay. A real Scottish woman suggests a place (after we've told her about the *eight minutes*) in a nearby village (beginning with 'F'), which boasts the oldest tree in Europe, or the pub down the road. Let's try the oldest-tree place, I say.

The hotel beginning with 'F' in the village which also claims to be the birthplace of Pontius Pilate (really), has a cherry tree outside in full bloom. There is a roaring fire with real peat. There is an antler chandelier. Comfy old sofas with tartan cushions everywhere, and a stuffed capercaillie in a glass vitrine. Big old floorboards that creak. It feels as if any minute Archie from *Monarch of the Glen* will charge downstairs, or Susan Hampshire will swan past in a Highland shawl fastened with a large heirloom brooch with entwined thistles on it. This was it!

But alas. No room at the inn. We tell the Scottish-*style* receptionist (not Scottish either) about the *eight minutes*. She cannot believe it. I like her. But still no room at the inn. They've been booked up for weeks. Probably nearly as long as we'd been booked up in the hotel beginning with 'A' (ending with 'g', nine letters).

'So, you didn't see *this* hotel on the web?' I meekly and meanly enquire of my choose-the-wrong-thing-again husband.

We limp back to the pub down the road.

'Rooms? No problem, mate!' (Not Scottish either.) We can even choose. Because every room is vacant. *How much?* Thirty quid. This Aussie gallant runs the bar, cooks, serves the food and takes guests to the rooms, all at the same time. All by himself. He runs around. *Yes, mate. Sure, mate. No problem, mate!* I like this place. I like him. I like the wonky windows in the room and I even like the view of the two mossy old caravans outside in the field. More Scottish-style to me. There's a clock radio. And milk. I'm happy here. It's a laugh. I hop into the shower. Sing. We're free! And we can eat any time we want! No problem, mate!

I get out of the shower. My smile fades. 'Oh no.'

'What?'

'Oh no.'

'What?'

'The ghosts.'

'What?'

'My pyjamas. Oh no . . .'

I realise I did not get my pyjamas when we made our escape. The ghosts at the hotel beginning with 'A' had hidden them under the sodding pillow. My all-time-favourite birthday pyjamas.

And then made the bed. So I couldn't see them. Or pack them. My going-away pyjamas. My comfortable sky-blue cotton pyjamas with the splattery pink dog roses. And now it's a long narrow windy road back, all the way round to the other side of the loch. It's miles. And tomorrow is our last day. And the last thing I want is to waste the morning driving back to the hotel. But at the same time, I don't want the hotel to get my favourite pyjamas. *I want my pyjamas.* I have never wanted them so much. Suddenly they have become irreplaceable. I look longingly out of the window, past the trailer homes, down the field and across the loch in the direction of the hotel. I wonder if there is a boat we can hire. Anything would be better than driving back.

We drown our sorrows at the bar. I tell our Aussie host about the very expensive hotel, beginning with 'A', ending in 'g', nine letters, south side of the loch (Tay), halfway down. I tell him about the *eight minutes*, about my birthday, about not being allowed in the dining room, about sitting on the naughty step.

His eyes spin into liquorice gobstoppers.

So I tell him about the cold triangles of tiny toast, and the refolded napkins, and the folded loo paper, and whisking the wine away, and the baby kippers, and the measly spots of butter, and the South African dictatorship and the telephone reminder calls.

'The Hotel A——?' he says, incredulous.

'The very same,' I nod.

'No!'

'I promise,' I nod.

'Wooaah . . . You're kidding me,' he says.

'I'm not.'

'Straight up?' he says. 'The bloody *expensive* Hotel A—?'

'Straight up. The very one.'

'Blimey!'

And then I tell him about my stranded pyjamas. How they were hidden under the pillow, and how they are my favourite pyjamas, and how I long to get them back, but how I cannot bear the idea of returning all the way back on the windy road, and how tomorrow is our last day, and now somebody – probably Badass – at the Hotel A— is going to get my beautiful birthday pyjamas. I ask him if we can hire a boat across the loch.

He roars and rubs his hands. 'Don't worry, mate. We'll get your pyjamas back. My boss is gonna *love* this!'

With that he leaps up and rushes to the kitchen. Through the swing doors we see him dialling a number. We fall silent as the Australian barman begins to regale John, owner of the pub beginning with 'L', about the couple who have just arrived: 'You'll never believe it, mate! They have just been . . . wait for it, mate, thrown out of . . . wait for it,' he cackles, 'the Hotel A—! Straight up. And you'll love this! Wait for it, wait for it. It was because they were eight minutes late for dinner! Heh, heh.' He roars with laughter. 'Yeah, that's what they said. God's truth, I'm telling you! Wouldn't let them in! Barred them! Yeah! Heh heh. And! Get this! It was her birthday! Barred on her birthday! Heh, heh.' He laughs some more. But I don't hear him mention anything about my pyjamas.

When he eventually comes back we order another pint.

'Will you *really* be able to get the pyjamas?' I ask hopefully.

'No problem, mate. Consider it done,' he says, chortling.

I would like a little more detail. How, and when exactly; but it feels ungracious to press him on it.

'Um, when, I mean how, um, would you get them?' I ask in a friendly, trying-to-be carefree way.

'Oh, I'll just go and get them.'

'Would you?' My little eyes sparkling.

'Yeah, sure.'

'Um, when . . . would you?'

He looks at me, a bit glazed now.

'It's just that, er, we're leaving tomorrow.'

'Ah, no problem, mate. I can post them then.'

'Really?' Eyes not quite so sparkling.

'Sure.'

At dinner (eight-thirty or was it nine?), two *huge* lamb shanks arrive on two huge plates. Each naked shin bone, presented erect, sticks out of its mound of marinated flesh with a sprig of rosemary sprouting from the top. It is a lone palm tree on a dessert island in a red ketchup sea. A nuclear bomb has gone off and here is the last atoll. The lumpy waves glimmer in a chemical sunset gleam.

'How's that?' our host enquires.

'Fantastic!' we chime.

He brings us each another climate-change island for dessert. An off-white sheet of icing crashes off an apple-pie-berg into, this time, a luminous sulphur-coloured sea. The red squiggles must be seal blood, or the last remnants of polar bears.

★

As we leave the next morning, I write down my address carefully, and insist on pressing a fiver for the postage into our Aussie barman's hand. To be fair, he doesn't want to take it. I know, deep down in my heart, he'll never stop by the no-rhododendron drive of the Hotel A—, let alone go in and ask for my pyjamas.

We visit the anything from two- to nine-thousand-year-old yew tree (conjecture varies); we stroll beside the beautiful Loch Tay; and four years later, we hear that the hotel beginning with A goes into administration, as the owner/chef – first name beginning with P, second name beginning with G and ending in S – scarpers back to South Africa. 'Suppliers rage as Loch Tay hotel boss bolts for South Africa' the *Daily Record* reports. 'Exclusive: AN AWARD-WINNING hotel is fighting for survival after its owner returned to his native South Africa leaving a trail of debt.'

I hope Sara told her husband how deeply disrespectful that was.

THE BLACK PURSE

We are going to the literature and music festival, Latitude. More civilised, Jonathan and I reckon, with the campervan – our tent days are over, but the dogs are not allowed to go, so we have sent an email out to all our friends and acquaintances to see if someone fancies a long weekend at our cottage in the country in return for looking after them.

That someone turns out to be Barbara and Bill and their two teenage sons, fourteen and sixteen, Lenster and Socrates. We have met a few times, Barbara is a writer and Bill is an actor. They would love a break from their small London flat and Barbara has some writing to finish. I am pleased because maybe this will help us get to know them a little better, as I have always been a little awkward with Barbara – a little nervous, my own paranoia and feelings of insecurity, I am sure. Bill and Lenster will be the forward party, arriving early for the instructions; Barbara and Socrates will join them the next day.

Bill and Lenster arrive. Hooray! We go through the dog food instructions, how to feed them, how much, when, where; the garden; the greenhouse watering; the keys; the fire; the hot water switch; the car parking; how the stove works; dishwasher; washing machine; there is a lot to take in. I change the sheets, put clean towels on the beds and maps and instructions out on the dining room table. Bill says that it will be a holiday from their busy lives, fresh air, walks and excursions to the pub, they can hardly wait. We have supper together, Lenster is funny and clever and curls up with the dogs. And so, in the morning, off we go.

When Jonathan and I arrive at the festival site, about six hours later, Latitude is a long queue of campervans to get into the top field, and then a long queue to the Ladies, and a long queue for the beer tent, where we have to pay £2 per plastic glass on top of the £7 per astronomical pint. And the clouds are building. Of course they are. There are queues everywhere you look, the venue tents are small, their capacity likewise, and there are a lot of people. And now we discover there is a ginormous commission at the ATMs, which shouldn't bother us, because I should have loads of cash, which I should have brought from home, which I had stashed away – almost a thousand pounds in notes, fifties, twenties, filling a black purse to bulging, which I was barely able to zip up. This unlikely amount, a quantity never before held in my hands let alone stuffed into one purse, was my earnings from my Christmas pop-up shop which had done surprisingly well in December, and instead of putting it in the bank I was using it as my own personal ATM. I kept the purse under my gloves in a small cupboard in the dining room, but now, as we pat our pockets to pay for our astronomically expensive beer, I realise with a sinking feeling that I have forgotten to bring any of it, and we will have to queue for the ATM and fork out the astronomical charges. But also, against my will, I cringe slightly, thinking of the unattended purse in the cupboard under the gloves. Not for a second do I think it won't be okay. But I chastise myself for my foolishness. I shouldn't have left it there. It is a preposterous thing to leave a purse lying around with a thousand quid in it. But I also tell myself not to worry, and I quickly move on and forget it.

And so we hang out at Latitude. And queue. And by the time we inch to the front, the first venue tent is full, and this happens again and again. And so we miss Simon Armitage, whose tent is full, and we miss Marcus Brigstocke, and we miss Ken Shuttleworth. And then I need to queue for the loo. And the Ladies queue is miles and miles, winding like a snake, like an airport queue except outside; and now it's begun to spit, so I join the 'just-peeing' queue, which is a quicker queue because you are given a cardboard funnel which is in fact a 'Shewee' – which means we can all pee together into a gutter, like the men. Which is actually quite a laugh, and maybe the highlight of Latitude for me, because I realise that I am not really a festival kind of person. I don't like queuing, for one thing, but here, even if I queue, I seem to miss everything. Jonathan goes to see Seasick Steve and says it was great, but I missed it because I was queuing for the Ladies. And when we do get to a stage in time, we have to stand and wait for hours as it gets more and more crowded, and our once good view is taken by more and more people who just barge in front of us. Then when Jonathan goes to the bar and has to queue for half an hour to buy two more seven-quid beers, he comes back telling me that a girl at the bar turned on him and said, 'It's Latitude, not Attitude!' I wonder how many times she's said that. When Paolo Nutini eventually comes on everyone just piles in front of us, and in front of me there is a girl with a big backpack on who is bopping and butting me every time she swings about. I move. But then another girl hops up on the shoulders of her boyfriend and I can't see a bloody thing. So we start grumbling and wondering why we bothered to pay £350 in entrance fees (a third of my hard-earned pop-up shop takings!) – a staggering amount, we feel, for being crushed and bumped and having to queue in the rain and pee into a cardboard funnel and park in the mud. We think of our garden and listening to music in the comfort of our own home, and we swear NEVER AGAIN.

The spitting has of course turned into a steady downfall. Now we are sloshing about. All the stalls begin selling umbrellas and Wellington boots for exorbitant prices. And all the events we wanted to see, like the dancing over the lake and the moth theatre, are cancelled because of the rain. Our expensive exclusive camper-van field is the furthest campsite from the main venues, and my feet hurt with all the walking back and forth, sliding and slipping past the sardine rows of tents with feet in muddy wellies sticking out under the fly sheets. Back in the campervan field, campervans are already getting stuck and their wheels are spinning round spraying mud like wet fireworks. And it is just horrible so instead of staying another night we decide to make a dash for it before everyone gets stuck and we are trapped here for days; they are already getting tractors in to haul stuck cars out. Jonathan, experienced with VWs from old surfing days and being a New Zealand farmer's son, says he knows what he is doing. And he does. He goes into tough driving mode, slip-sliding the accelerator, knowing just how fast to go and where to drive, and where not to – unlike our fellow campers, who are quickly getting bogged down. I am gripping the dashboard as a VW in front of us chooses the wrong direction and grinds into the mud. We skid slightly, speed up and slew around a corner. In the mirror we see the van behind us stuck up to its axles. Yay, not us! We are away! We are not trapped in the campervan field in the rain or waiting for the tractor or queuing for the Ladies or tapping digits into the ATM. So we go to a pub to celebrate with normal-priced beer and delicious crab sandwiches. And then we drive three hours to visit our friends Jane and Adrian in Sussex and drink a lot of wine and stay the night, and then we drive three hours home. By which time Bill and Barbara have left because the kids need to be back for school, and the dogs are in the garden as agreed, with (rather strangely) the kitchen chairs, out in the rain.

Hooray, it is good to be home, rain or no rain, wet chairs or dry! But we can't find the key. Bill must have confused the hiding place. But eventually we locate the key and open the door to find a bottle of vodka and a thank-you note on the dining room table from Bill, with their news, their outings, their Sunday tea at Wimborne St Giles, the dogs being sweet; they have had a good time and there is a sense about the place that *feels* like they have had a good time. The al fresco (damp) kitchen chairs, books down from the shelves; even the chessboard has had an outing. There are the dregs of a happy atmosphere, the towels are on the line, board games from the shed are in the house, books from the house are in the shed. And we are relieved that everything seems to have gone so well.

Three days later I need some cash. But the purse is not in its place in the small cupboard under the gloves. After the initial moment of discovery, when I feel like I have just swallowed a chest freezer, my hands panic, throwing the gloves aside, throwing everything out of the cupboard, and I stare disbelievingly at the pile on the floor, which does not include the black purse. It is impossible. It is *so* impossible that I had completely forgotten about it and didn't even check when we got home. I put my hot cheeks into my cold hands and stop breathing. I start breathing and search, going through everything again. It must be obscured by something, trapped between something. I can hardly form the words: the purse has gone. Maybe they pulled it out, looking for games, and put it somewhere, forgot where it lived. I search our tiny house from top to bottom. There are only five rooms, so it doesn't take long. I search again. I take the house apart, look under cushions, behind the loo, everywhere. I know it was there, it was always there, I only had one hiding place for the purse. Through the cushions again, under the beds, in every drawer, up, under, on, beneath, down the back of. There are only so many places you can search in a two-bedroom house. The purse is nowhere.

One day goes by. I tell Jonathan. He searches in all the same places (but not as thoroughly). Another day. I cannot sleep for trying to work it out, for the mystery, for the disbelief, and the worrying about what to do. Say nothing? Ask? Say nothing? But it is a *thousand* pounds. Not fifty. Not a hundred and fifty.

Bill and Barbara are not well off, they both work hard, and they have a lot of outgoings, two strapping sons, one of whom is soon to go to university, with the other hard on his heels. I go through every permutation and Jonathan and I talk endlessly about what to do.

Our imaginations fly about. But what if? And which one? It is just *impossible*. Round and round. But deep down I know we have to ask. We cannot carry on *not* asking. There might, after all, be a simple explanation. But how to bring it up without the whiff of accusation? And then there is that other thing, the unsayable, the horrible creeping feeling that we might, *might* have been taken for a ride. A person who has a thousand pounds in a purse – at one level it's fairly bad taste, leaving a purse lying around like that stuffed to the gunnels with notes. My mind continues to spin with possibilities and impossibilities. The boys? We didn't meet Socrates, but Lenster was unimpeachable. He loved the dogs. How could a boy who loved dogs be responsible? Or could a wad of bank notes prove too much temptation even for him? On the face of it, we had a cottage with a big garden and a campervan, and a purse full of money. An unimaginable amount. Monopoly money. All the things they could do with it. Don't go there, don't go there. Socrates is just about to begin university and summer is coming and all his friends are going to Greece while he has to get a job over the holidays. I really don't think that even all this temptation would be enough. But maybe. Maybe it happened in a flash, bang, it's in his hands, the match is struck, the deed is done. And then the idea of having it begins to nestle so sweetly, until the repercussions slide away. It could help so much. It could do so much! It is theirs. We have plenty. And then it's too late. No. No. No. They were too smart, too clever, too nice. The younger one? Impossible. The elder? No! But then again . . . A moment of madness, a tiny puff of mischief that turned into something else, something he couldn't return from? What I was capable of at sixteen I wouldn't like to say. I remember nicking a china swan from a shop for my mum's birthday, my only worry was if I were caught, for the shop had plenty of ornaments.

I drive Jonathan crazy, returning to it over and over. What do you think? Who do you think? Questions that, as each day passes, look like they will never be answered.

Then another thought takes hold. A nasty despicable thought. Don't think it. Don't think it. Barbara. Barbara has this sort of dignified manner that one looks up to, but at the same time is slightly cautious of. She is a writer, a writer who is published (as I wouldn't mind being). An explorer into the human psyche, into its mysteries and complications. She is respected and reviewed and asked to talk publicly and do writerly things. Which is another reason why this is so fucking awful. She is the distiller of Experience, the wordsmith; I'm the wannabe, riddled with discomfort and failings. At a party Barbara once asked me (she asked me, no one ever asked me) about the book I was slaving over. I imagine I looked eager – or, God forbid, grateful – and then she huskily whispered, 'So tell me, what *exactly* would you say is the emotional core of your novel?' Fuck. The *emotional* core? With the emphasis on the *exactly*.

The idea of putting everything I had been thinking about into one neat response paralysed me. My whole story spiralled down the plug. I needed a fine-tuned, one-sentence reply at the ready, and I didn't have one. She waited. It was a test, and I was a galumphing heffalump. She understood not just the power of words, but the power of withholding them. I said something idiotic. Stuttering, tongue-tied and banal. She looked disappointed. Of course she did.

Dare I say it, dare I think it . . . Barbara has fine tastes. We know this, even though we do not know Barbara well, because we bumped into her once, sitting outside Carluccio's near Brunswick Square, and she had a balloon of very expensive cold white Burgundy with the bottle in the ice bucket, and a plate of antipasta, salamis and meats, and a bowl of giant olives, the enormous gourmet kind, the kind that costs you an arm and a leg. It struck me at the time as an expensive snack for an impecunious writer on the virtual breadline. Barbara frequents tasteful establishments, and wears elegant clothes, and, and . . . so I enter the dark cave-network of suspicion. Are we being laughed at? Because she knows we will never dare to ask? Oh God, our mutual friends, the discomfort . . . Stop it. STOP IT! What about Bill? No, Bill is funny, self-deprecating, imaginative, surprising; this scenario just doesn't have legs.

I know we have to ask. A week has passed and every night I toss and turn as my paranoia multiplies. I search the house again, countless times I return to the cupboard and look under the gloves.

So we decide to call Bill. But we will do so carefully, very,

very carefully and very diplomatically. I will call. I will say how difficult it is to ask, and that I hope he will understand, and how embarrassed I am, and that we know there is a perfectly good explanation, but that we have to ask, because something happened on 'their watch' and we are completely stumped, and we need to unravel it.

So I do. I call Bill and I say how unfortunate and uncomfortable it is, but I have to ask a difficult question, and that *please* don't misconstrue it (whatever that means) and that we are in no way accusing anyone, but we are mystified and need to check all lines of enquiry (ugh, I sound like a politician), and without meaning any offence, if he could find a way of finding out if anyone can remember seeing it . . . ? Bill is silent. Steely silent. And stupidly I fill the infernal silence up: moment of madness, blah, blah; when I was young I got up to all sorts of stuff; a mistake that couldn't be undone . . . Bill says efficiently that he will ask the boys.

I put down the phone. Not great. Not really how I had planned things in my head. But nevertheless I have at least shared the burden, I have passed the problem on. Fifteen minutes later the phone rings. It's Bill. His voice is clear and concise. He has asked Socrates and Lenster and they didn't take it. He could tell by their faces, he says. What, he just asked them outright? That wasn't what I meant at all. I didn't want him to ask his kids if they had stolen our money. I am appalled. I'd hoped he would be more subtle, investigative, less hurtful, talk to Barbara, maybe even have a look in the boys' bedroom, see if there were any new purchases. I don't know what I wanted, or what I expected, but not this. He asks me to let him know if I find it. I tell him I will. But his tone is cold and hurt, you bet it is. I search the house again. Nothing. I search the sheds. Nothing. I wait for Barbara to ring, for surely she must have been told and will want to sort it out. To talk it through. What could have happened to it? But she doesn't. Day after day, no call. And we are left to stew. I sweat and lie awake in bed. Oh God, what have we done? Or what has been done to us? It is one or the other, it has to be. A week. Another week. Silence. I search the house again. And again.

I knew a very respectable kleptomaniac once. She was a bookish highly educated woman who led her friends a merry song and dance, stealing from them. She was quite content to let others take the blame for her misdemeanours and borrowings: rings, precious family heirlooms, money, knick-knacks. Her boyfriend's mother sacked their cleaner on account of so many disappearances. Eventually she was caught by her best friend, who became suspicious and laid a trap. It is a disease that grabs hold of you apparently, like gambling. It starts small then grows with every success, you make all sorts of justifications for it: you are liberating things; others have things unfairly; you have a right; you rationalise your wrongdoing. One of my friends once nicked a duvet from John Lewis. A duvet! And got caught. Of course. Quilty or not quilty. Some kleptomaniacs even accept their thievery as a kind of artistic exploration into nether worlds. They get used to it. Could Barbara be researching a character for a novel? I have stopped thinking it might be Lenster or Socrates. It is Barbara. That's why she hasn't rung us. It explains why sometimes she slid past not recognising you, making her way to wherever she wanted to be. I see it now. I wake at night thinking about it. It goes round and round.

By now of course it is out. And massaged into a massive drama. We are the offenders. We have accused Bill and Barbara's children of stealing our money. We have hurt their family to the core. Everyone is shocked. And I am pissed off because so far all we have done is ask. I call our mutual friend, Rob. Rob thinks we should never have said anything. That we should have just left it. Really? Just take it on the chin? Yes, he says. And you think I should just leave it now? Not say anything? Yes, he says, that's what he would do. But it's not what I would do. I want to solve it, and clear my head, and make it better. I certainly don't want to be the villain in all this. I suggest I write a nice email to Bill and Barbara, and that I send it to him to check first.

And so I do. I spend hours over it, and Rob tweaks it so it is as soft as peach velvet, and I step into their shoes, so that hopefully they can step into ours, so that we can try and work out what happened. And Rob says it's okay, so swish – out it goes – and BANG! within the hour a reply straight back. From Naples, from their holiday (another one?), which I have interrupted, and which I am ruining: THEY DO NOT HAVE OUR PURSE! And that is that. The End. But of course it is not the end.

★

I am not thinking about any of it, thank goodness, which has been rare over the last few weeks, for it keeps flipping back into my head, like sour butter churning round and round – the fallout and the unsolved mystery. No, I am washing up, looking out of the kitchen window, when I see a man I don't recognise walking down the garden path. Behind him, tentative, hanging back, a teenage boy. I go out to meet them. Not a delivery, but probably someone lost up our lane. The man pushes the boy forward. He says they have something to give me. The boy's face is pale, which exaggerates the rash across his neck, he has liquid, see-through eyes and slightly greasy bark-coloured hair. And fiddly fingers. The teenage boy passes me the black purse. I look down at the purse that fills my hand. My eyes prick with tears, even though I do not believe them. I am completely speechless for a moment which feels longer, probably, than it is. I am making peculiar un-word-like noises. The man nudges the boy. The boy says he is sorry. That's all. His eyes fall to the brick path and stay there, while my eyes flick from boy to man to purse to man to ask the man the questions. He says he hopes the money is all there. And then he gives me my mother's gold bracelet – which I had not even noticed was missing. I am literally dumbstruck as he tells me that his son, for this is who he is, made a big mistake, a prank that went wrong, with his friend, a few Sundays ago. They had been exploring, cycling down the lane; it was a dare, his father said, to nick something from somewhere, a shed or an open garage, and there was no one around, but apparently there was a window open . . . And while his son waited, his friend hopped in.

Yes! There was a window open, I remember now how the sash window had been left open in the sitting room. I closed it when we arrived home. The man is extremely uncomfortable. The man's wife had found the purse after first discovering three £50 notes in the boy's bedroom. It took them a while to extract the information. I want to hug the man. And the boy. But the boy does not want to be here. He is looking at the bricks in the path. His foot is going back and forth, grinding something under his shoe. It is excruciating for him. But not for me. It is a blessed relief, this release from all the awful thoughts of treachery and deceit that have been marauding around my head and keeping me awake at night. And all my questions congeal into a knot of gratefulness. I am almost speechless, but at the same time I hear words coming out, half-formed sentences, about how relieved I am, and how terrible it has been, and, and, and . . . I can tell that the boy *really* does not want to be here, nor the man. They are under duress. So all I can do is thank them. I am in a mad thanking frenzy. Thank you, thank you. Almost, thank you for stealing my purse. Thank you that it is not Barbara or Socrates or Lenster. Thank you for coming. Thank you for having the courage and moral fortitude to come. For the miracle. Thank you God (almost) that the person who stole my purse had decent parents, a father who brought his son back, who made it right, who has given his son something he will remember all his life. I am overwhelmed with disbelief and thankfulness. I could kiss the boy. And the father. I have to stop myself. I am thanking them and thanking them and telling the boy how brave he is, and that it has caused SO MUCH TROUBLE, but now, because he has done this brave thing, I can right it all. I nearly open the purse and pay him. But I know that would not be the right thing. The father and son want to get this over as quickly as possible and be gone. They turn to leave. And I want to ask a million things, but my mind goes blank and I am so overflowing with gratefulness that I follow them out to their small silver car, watch them turn, and wave them goodbye. Our neighbour, Tony, appears, and it all gushes out and he is amazed. Then our other neighbour, Terry, walks past and the story gushes out again. Terry remembers seeing two boys on bikes, the weekend of the motocross, acting suspiciously and then zooming back down the lane at breakneck speed.

I can't wait to tell Barbara. I ring her straight away. Her mobile ringing tone goes to that continental *brrrr, brrrr, brrrr, brrrr*. Still on holiday, then. My heart is beating with happiness and excitement. Everything is going to be all right. The phone picks up. Hello! I am so eager to tell her that I blurt it out without preamble, how a man and boy appeared in the garden, but Barbara cuts me off quickly. What do I want? I tell her the purse has turned up! But before I can explain, she cuts me off.

'I am glad you *found* your money,' she says curtly.

I am confused by her word choice. Although I am wrong-footed I start to relate the story, of the man and the boy suddenly appearing in the garden, but she cuts me off again. They are on holiday and busy and she needs to go. What she is making very clear is that she is *not* interested. I am the child-accuser. The phone goes to dialling tone. My elation slumps. It is too late. The damage has been done. There will be no stepping into each other's shoes. As far as she is concerned I suspected her innocent children of the most heinous crime. She is pissed off. And will remain so. And, frankly, who can blame her?

So, naturally, I do begin to blame her. After all, they went out for tea and left the bleeding window *wide* open; it was open when we arrived home, and our kitchen chairs were out in the rain, and the backgammon and chess boards were all moved about and not put back, *and* the key was in the wrong place, and, and, and worse, she had never called us back, even if it was just to talk it through. No, I shouldn't have said anything, Rob was right, it would have all sorted itself out, without them ever knowing. I fucked up big time.

And it is not the end for Barbara either, because what filters back is that she is convinced I have made the whole story up. That the black purse was never lost in the first place. Or there was no purse. I just decided to accuse them. Barbara doesn't believe me. Barbara has never believed me. Teach me to mess with a mother and her children. So I email Barbara. Yes, I do, I still want to try to make amends. I say I can only imagine how horrible it must have been for them and that I am SO SORRY and I apologise and scrape. I am so sorry and I was careless of her feelings. I want to make it better. I really do. Because I hate bad feeling and we see each other, not all the time, but at social events sometimes. I hate not being able to defend myself, and somehow I feel it's all my fault, because it certainly isn't theirs. And also because there the unlanced carbuncle sits, ugly, throbbing, suppurating in my head, and each time I think about it, it is toe-curlingly bad, and not getting any better. Nothing. Two days, three days, a week.

Until at last, my email is coolly acknowledged. But it is clear that the offence committed and the offence taken is fixed.

Back I go into my writing shed, tap, tapping away, trying to get on with it, deleting, trying again, deleting. Meanwhile, Barbara's new novel is published. How brilliant it is, everyone says. I hear her interviewed on the radio. I see her handsome face in the papers. I see (but don't read) her glowing reviews. Then I hear she is on the longlist for a most prestigious prize. Then she is on the shortlist. I imagine being woken up by Barbara being interviewed on the *Today* programme. Then paraded all over the front pages. Beaming out. My guilt is stalking me, and there is a great big rub-your-nose-in-it judge in the sky. No rising above it, not big enough. If only there was a way to make the impending possibility of Barbara's win bearable . . .

Ha. I go online. I click on William Hill. And I put a hundred pounds on Barbara to win.

THE GOOD UNCLE

India. Neither Jonathan nor I have ever been. 'You've never been to India?' our Australian friend, Trevor, exclaims. But where on earth (or in India) should one begin? We tend to gravitate to places away from people, not towards billions of them. I've seen pictures of the streets. It looks hectic. And hot. Trevor says we will be sissies if we go to Goa and lie on the beach. That isn't really India. I make a lame attempt to read up. Mark Tully begins *No Full Stops in India* with the reply he gives to people who ask him how he deals with the poverty: he says he doesn't have to deal with it, the poor do. Günter Grass *witnesses* India with words and drawings: fast ink-splat pen-work across the page – bones, cows, crows pile up in the refuse heap, circles of drying dung decorate walls. 'Ignore the misery,' he wrote. 'Custom invites you to ignore it.' I get the guidebooks, doorstoppers of leaden prose full of names I've never heard of. In the library I find a photograph in a book on Rajasthan of an ornate carriage drawn by two deer. Trevor thinks we should begin, *no messing*, in Varanasi. So gladly I put the books away. Our main debate becomes whether to splash out and get a driver, but that feels like a cop out, and so middle class.

Varanasi, holy city, city of temples, city of pilgrims, is famous, amongst many things, for its ghats – successions of wide stone stairs leading down to the holy river, the Ganges. I make Jonathan come with me to Manikarnika Ghat, which is famous for being the main cremation ghat, where funeral pyres glow day and night, and bodies wrapped in shrouds queue up on biers beside enormous stacks of wood. Wood is very expensive, but to be cremated on the banks of the Ganges is auspicious for the next life as it bestows instant liberation from the cycle of life and death. I'm curious to see a burning hand or foot. Jonathan is more interested in the bloated dead dog in the river, gliding amongst chrysanthemum petals just next to a young boy cleaning his teeth. We sit on the stone steps and wait.

How *very fortunate* we are, a whispering man who has appeared from nowhere tells us. We have a great opportunity. A karmic chance. A blessing of good luck from the holy river, he tells us, because we can help the Waiting to Die. The man's dark eyes bore into our pale eyes. He points upwards. The Waiting to Die are waiting to die in the building right beside the cremation ghat. I look up at the stark, ominous Waiting to Die building. Huge and square and overbearing and derelict-looking, its concrete walls zigzagged with stained cracks. I pale. But how can *we* help the Waiting to Die? We can visit them. Oh no, please don't make us. He knows we have come to watch the burning bodies. The accusation is in his stare. He beckons. I *really* don't want to go. Certainly not *right* this minute. I want to stay and see a burning body. We have only just arrived. Yet to refuse, in favour of watching his fellow countrymen burn, feels, well, shameful. He is very insistent. Jonathan is giving me the eye. He seems to think we *should* visit the Waiting to Die. Jonathan follows the beckoning whispering man. I plod after them. An invisible chain binds us as we are led from spooky room to spooky room. Plod, plod. Everything is bare and stone-coloured: skin, wood, stone. An emaciated old woman sits by the window looking out; another lies on a hard wooden pallet, her bony hand held out for money for wood, like a little bird claw. Blood bangs in my ears. Serves me right. My clot of shame trampling in their death-dust. Plod, plod. Another room. Bony smiles and outstretched bony hands. Plod, plod. More dust, more hands. Bugger this. I pirouette around on my heel, don't even bother to tell Jonathan, and flee. I speed-walk back the way we came, past the skeleton women on the broken cradle, past the outstretched hands, kicking up the stone-coloured dust as I escape the building, leaving Jonathan to the whispering man.

I wait for him at the ghat where there is a burning baby and a naked *sadhu*. In seconds, I am surrounded by children, big children, small children, entrepreneurs in the making: *Where you from? Where you going tomorrow? Where you going now? You have ticket? How much you buy ticket?*

Eyes, so many eyes.

At dawn we take a riverboat to watch the sunrise. Shoals of petals and armadas of candles in tiny coracles float past. Jonathan is aghast when I say, at the boatman's inquisition, that we have two children. Daughters. 'Eight—' I begin, until I realise I shouldn't have left such young children at home, and clumsily change it to eight-*teen*, and nineteen. The boatman smiles. Content. It felt weird, Jonathan tells me later. But I say it was easier to deflect the interrogation than have to explain ourselves and be sold lucky stones, or blame God, or meet those saucer eyes. But there was also, if I am honest, a brief sweet moment of parenthood – eighteen and nineteen, mooncalves.

Along the banks, children scavenge the ashes for gold teeth and wedding rings. Dogs fight over black meat. Trees are dressed in living monkeys and paper kites.

After hours of agonising we decide. (Three days in Varanasi might have helped.) At Agra we are getting a driver. He will meet us off the train. A driver from Delhi to drive us around and wait for us while we see things.

'So what will he do when we're, I don't know, looking at a palace?' I ask Jonathan.

'He'll wait.'

'What, just wait?'

'Yes.'

'Just wait for us? In the car?'

'Yes, that's what you pay for.'

'What, for hours?'

'Yes. However long it takes.'

'Oh, what, every day he drives us around and waits for us, for *two whole weeks*, like Lord and Lady Muck?'

'It's his job,' Jonathan tells me.

'That's going to make us feel really great, isn't it?'

'That's how it is.'

I can't see the point of having a feeling-guilty holiday.

'And where does he sleep? In the car?'

'They have drivers' accommodation.'

'But he doesn't know where we want to go yet.'

'All these places have rooms where the drivers sleep.'

'How do you know?'

'Because I do. It's all catered for. Look, it's different here. It's a job. It's a good job. They want to work. They *need* to work. We are employing them. Or do you want to catch a bus? You want to catch a bus all over Rajasthan with your bag? Have you clocked the buses? We need a driver if we are going to see things properly. If we want to get off the beaten track.'

'So, he is just going to be there, away from his family, twenty-four hours a day at our beck and call?'

'Yes.'

It feels preposterous, but we decide on it all the same. We book a driver, but not a posh car, not one of those nice Morris Oxford saloon cars – an economy car, without aircon.

It is with some relief that we board the night train at Varanasi Junction, and find our second-class carriage. The close proximity of our fellow passengers, a family of six, is strangely liberating. Eight of us, three bunks on each side and two at the end. Plus the other members of their family who join us for supper from further up the train. For the next thirteen hours we share our air, front passage, back passage. The father regularly lifts a cheek high off the seat to satisfyingly break wind. We sip sweet *chai* and rock along. Or pad up the train to the eye-smarting Indian-style loo, where a sticky stainless-steel hole frames the Indian continent flashing by. I traverse it like a spider, keeping my body as far away from everything as I can, bury my nose in my sleeve, then crouch down. After we have been put to bed by the train-bunk wallah, from under my railway blanket I spy on the father in the opposite bunk. His mouth is a fat rosebud of trapped air. It swells like a blister, then bursts. Seven instruments in the orchestra of this carriage. Trumpet for a bottom, oboe for a mouth. The snores are so loud there are times I burst out laughing, like a child.

★

Our train pulls into Agra station at dawn. As we look out across the sea of people on the platform and wonder how we will ever find our driver, there's a voice in the train's corridor heading straight for our carriage, calling 'Mr Jonathan, Mr Jonathan'. It is Ajai, our driver, with whom we will spend the next two weeks. The moment I see Ajai, I am filled with an overwhelming gladness. He is young, twenty-three or twenty-four, his clean white teeth flashing in tandem with his pressed cotton shirt.

Ajai's not-a-Morris-Oxford is a white Nissan Sunny, a two-door hatchback. Our luggage overflows from the boot onto the back seat. *No problem, no problem.* We squeeze in. He is *very happy* to be our driver, *very happy.* We are very happy too, we tell him.

Indeed, we couldn't be happier as we drive off, safe, protected, enwombed in Ajai's Nissan Sunny, towards the Taj Mahal. What a contrast already. Varanasi, holy city, city of pyres, burden on the senses, altar of the imagination, streaming away in our exhaust trail; flowing away with the holy river in the billowing smoke from the cremation fires, with the orange petals, and dead dogs, and charred pelvises. What a relief. Hooray. No more self-appointed guides. No more compromising situations.

And so, after Ajai waits for us for the whole morning at the Taj Mahal, we set off to drive across Rajasthan. Within ten minutes of beginning our journey he turns off the main road, and suddenly we are outside the door of a souvenir shop, *Enjoy, enjoy.* The owner has been waiting for us. He welcomes us with a voice as warm as ripe fruit. I look at the rows of statues and carvings and soapstone ashtrays and my happy fluid mood sets like jelly and my expression sets like soapstone, and we don't buy anything, and back in the car I tell Ajai we don't want to go to souvenir shops. He looks uncomfortable. He says it is his job. We say it is his job to drive us around. Ajai explains he will get into trouble if he doesn't take us to the souvenir shops because his boss tells him to take us there, and we realise we are on the two-door-no-aircon-souvenir-shop-stop-super-economy package. We tell Ajai to call his boss and say that we are a very awkward couple who refuse to go to souvenir shops, and if we are taken to souvenir shops again, we will cancel the trip. Ajai says he will talk to his boss. And we set off again, Ajai's Indian pop music playing, the windows open and dust billowing everywhere.

Our first destination is the wildlife sanctuary of Bharatpur, famed for its birds – and, I read somewhere, tigers! Which is why we've decided to come here instead of the more famous wildlife park, Ranthambhore, because there will be fewer tourists. And there *are* fewer tourists. I am not sure where I got this tiger information from, because the last tiger in the park was a poor fleabitten old thing who died decades ago. The only tigers we see at Bharatpur are on the walls of our hotel in black and white photographs – and lifeless, beneath the booted feet of Raj princes and their pith-helmeted colonial white guests. We decide to explore the park on bicycle, which we can hire with a guide at the entrance. But when we tell our tall, thin, allocated guide that we want him for two or three hours, after which we want to explore on our own, he is almost suicidal. He has been waiting four days in the queue for his turn. *Bad luck, very bad luck*, he shakes his head, for he cannot earn enough money in three hours to look after his family. *No, no, not to worry*, even though only he is a proper ornithologist, and there are too many guides – who are *not* proper ornithologists, and there is not enough work to go around, and he will have to go to the back of the queue, and it might be a whole week until it is his turn again, and his mother is in hospital waiting for an operation, and if she doesn't have the operation she will die, like his brother who died only a few months ago, and his mother is heartbroken, and this is the only money he will earn to pay for the operation, and to pay for his family to live, and his wife is sick as well, and we are not to worry.

We glumly ride our clanking bikes with wobbly seats along the paths of the wildlife sanctuary, following our bone-thin, downtrodden, unappreciated ornithologist. We see a few deer, a few birds, and some eagle-owl chicks in a nest – which is good, but there has been a drought in this park for some years, so now there are fewer birds, and fewer animals, he explains. Nevertheless, there are rows of stone plaques etched with long lists that hint how many there used to be. On 31 January 1913, *HON'BLE Mr MONTAGUE* bagged 2,122 birds with forty guns; on 3 December 1914, *H.E. Viceroy Lord HARDING* bagged 4,062 with forty-nine guns; and in 1916, *Lord CHELMSFORD, on the occasion of his visit,* blew 4,206 brief feathery lives out of the sky with fifty guns; and there are rather a lot of these names on these plaques, and a vast amount of numbers.

In contrast to our heavily tipped bicycle guide, Ajai could not be more cheerful, affable, or happy with his lot. We feel very lucky indeed. The souvenir shop blip is forgotten. It is hard to imagine a more likeable driver. He seems completely at ease with us, as we are with him. Each day Ajai likes to practise English words as we drive along. *Tin-opener, business enterprise, washing-up, fluffy dice, corkscrew, salary, weather forecast, what time is lunch, is it boring?, refuse collection, coriander.* But Jonathan is called *Mr Jonathan*, and I am *Madam*, and some things are fixed, however hard we try.

And for the next two weeks this becomes our life. Ajai waits for us while we visit enormous forts and opulent palaces and wildlife parks. He assures us he is happy to do this – *Enjoy!* – and that this is his job. And we get very accustomed to having a driver at our beck and call. We tell him we could not imagine a better driver. And we cannot. Except when he pretends to know the way and refuses to ask and we drive miles in the wrong direction, and I keep asking if this is the right way, and he says *yes, it is the right way, madam*, because he is too proud to turn around. But he does have the measure of us. 'Would we like go rat temple? Very few tourists and many, many rats.' 'Oh yes, a rat temple, yes, please,' we say. And there *are* a million rats, dead rats, live rats, floating rats, baby rats, tame rats, and very, very large rats, swarming through the crumbling ruins and swimming across the fetid pools, with hardly anyone around, except for a very grubby holy man who lures us into a tight corner, and presses his red thumb onto our foreheads leaving a circle of henna like a third eye. We stupidly bow our thanks, but the blessing, or curse or whatever it is, is not of course a gift, but a transaction, and the rupee notes which Jonathan gives him are not enough. Holy man is very angry. We pat our pockets. Holy man is shouting at us. We run away.

'Enjoy?' Ajai asks expectantly, as we arrive at the car.

'Oh yes, thank you Ajai.'

Ajai is a miracle. Every morning, clean white shirt and smiling face. He tells us his wife in Delhi is expecting their first child.

'You want a boy or girl, Ajai?'

'Oh, boy,' he smiles.

Ajai and his wife live with Ajai's mother, and his elder brother, Hrithik. Ajai's father died when he was sixteen. Ajai's brother works in a bank and is *very highly qualified*. Ajai is extremely proud of his brother. Hrithik's English is *very very good*, not like Ajai's, Ajai says. Ajai's sister is *married to man in Bikaner*. Ajai's *marriage was love marriage*. His sister's was *arranged marriage*. Ajai's mother, I am shocked to learn, is younger than me.

It is good fun driving with Ajai. *Chillies, wedding, pickled, fair, I have cut myself, colonial power, beautiful actress, sieve, wild flower, economy, mutiny, pillion, chewing gum, global warming, moustache.* We tell Ajai we don't want to eat where the tourists eat and where the Morris Oxfords park. We want to eat at the roadside stops where Indians eat. And so we do. We have curry dhal and rice at dusty shacks, sitting on upturned crates, encircled by small bands of children. We are watched like a tennis match, they close in, then run away again. They have a mischievous quality I like. Skinny-limbed; big toothy smiles; little grown-ups. There are children I'd like to take home with me. Or maybe just their easy joy. A tiny bottle of hotel shampoo thrills them. I tell them not to drink it. You can easily loathe yourself here.

As each mile goes past, *camel, barber, refrigerator, dead dog,* India works its way across our eyes, our skin, our thinking. And defecation is in my thinking a lot. Shit, and the passing thereof. It's omnipresent, people ducking down, straddling their buttocks over a ditch, in the street, next to their market stall. Each morning the fields are sown with people *in flagrante delicto*. Here, there, everywhere, a polka-dot technique. No long-drop. No latrine. And while everything is cheap in India, little is free, except dust, so I can't help wondering why there is no commerce in shit. Five to six hundred million freshly laid evacuations a day. Soft brown buns. Strictly vegetarian. In England, in the 1900s, outdoor privies were emptied into pits, layered with ash or lime and dug out by the men in the village once a year, then spread across the allotments. They called it black gold. So I cannot for the life of me work out why, in a land of so many businessmen, there is no business in this. I try to discuss it with Ajai, in a delicate way.

'Ajai, why does everyone, um, why don't they, er . . . you know, because there are no, um, er, bathrooms, and the people have to go, er, outside, so, why don't they collect it in one place, then use it as fertiliser for the fields?'

He nods sideways.

'You know? Food for vegetables,' I explain. 'Is it for religious reasons?' I suggest.

He nods sideways again. I tell Ajai I am not sure what the sideways nod means. Is it *yes* or *no* or *don't know*, or is it ironic? Does it express some kind of discomfort, or disagreement?

'What you mean, sideways?' he asks.

I don't like to do the nod myself, but now I must. I do it

quickly, sort of wobble my head. Jonathan is looking at me, and by his expression, I can tell, not very impressed.

'I don't know,' Ajai says. Then he says his brother, Hrithik, is *very good businessman, very highly qualified.*

In Pushkar we try to find some peace and walk away from the town. We take a track through a plantation of rose bushes. A flock of children follow us, *Rupee, rupee.* Barefooted ragamuffins. We tell them we have no rupees and walk on, but nothing deters them, they whoosh around us like a wave around a rock. *Rupee, rupee.* Behind us, in front of us. We give them sweets. They don't want sweets, *Rupee, rupee.* We quicken our pace. We just want half an hour, *half an hour*, to ourselves. We walk doggedly on and eventually shake most of them off. Except one. A tiny, skinny, persistent girl, dust-blended skin, hair in a matted lump. *Rupee, rupee mister, fifty, fifty.*

'Fifty!' We walk on.

She pops up in front of us. *Rupee, rupee.* Then beetles off to intersect us at the bottom of the field. Now she has a rose to sell us. *Rupee, rupee*, she holds out the rose. We shake our heads. Oh God, we do. A horrible slow patronising NO shake. Yet she pesters us all the way back; her tenacity is incredible, but we don't give in. Not even at the bitter end as she reaches the end of her track and watches us disappear into town. I think of this girl at night, between my clean white sheets, her large liquid eyes, trying everything, not giving up, trying to sell us her stolen rose. What have I become?

★

215

India does not shut up. She whispers in your head. All day. Worries at you. You even – yes! – try to work her out. Even when you laugh at yourself for doing so. Then you realise you have begun to call her *her*. Where does one begin with India? Too big, too broken, too holy. Too too. Why would one begin at all? Because she won't roll over. Because at night your dreams are techni-coloured, because infuriating, unwieldy, tormenting as she is, she gnaws away at you. Because she lays a million eyes on your tawdry soul.

In Jaipur we grind to a halt in a funnel of traffic, a man walks past bent double with a sack (the size of a baby elephant) of rose petals on his back.

Sometimes Ajai is happy with his accommodation and some-times he is not. Every hotel so far, as Jonathan predicted, provides a room for the drivers and a meal. I interrogate Ajai each morning on the quality of his board and ask him to give it a mark out of ten. Sometimes he just jiggles his head sideways (I'm still not sure what this means). But today there is no holding back.

'Accommodation very bad.'

'Oh no. Why?'

'Very bad.'

'Why? How, Ajai?'

'Very dirty.'

'Really?'

'Very dusty.'

'Oh dear.'

'Not even a room,' he says. 'What is it called? For a horse?'

'A stable,' I say.

'I am not a horse.'

'No, Ajai. You are not a horse.'

This is bad news. Because we like this hotel very much indeed. Rohet Garh is our one taste of luxury, of dilapidated luxury, but luxury nevertheless. We want to stay two more nights and stop looking at forts, so we can swim in the marble swimming pool, and drink gin and tonic on the veranda, and dine outside on the terrace under the marble porticos, and cavort about in our ginormous room. There is a lake, and peacocks, and rattan chairs all over the lawn and Bruce Chatwin stayed here for a whole winter writing *The Songlines*, and they have said I can ride one of their beautiful white Marwari horses with the strange curly ears.

'What do we do about Ajai?' I ask Jonathan.

'There's nothing we can do.'

'Should we talk to someone?'

'You must be joking,' he says, looking at me as if I'm mad. 'They won't do anything. He can go off for a couple of days if he wants. He'll be fine.'

At dusk, the ghostly meowings of peacocks falling from trees.

The beauty of the hotel outweighs the discomfort of thinking about the discomfort of Ajai. And I try not to think about him as we glide about, and swim in the marble pool with a blue lotus flower mosaic on the bottom, and sip gin and tonic in rattan chairs, amongst potted palms and sepia photographs of maharajahs and dead tigers. In *The Hindu Times* I read about the new roaring trade in surrogacy – because adoption is a long and laborious process, and to qualify you have to adhere to the Hindu faith. There are 44 million destitute children in India, and 12 million in orphanages.

I go for a ride with the groom who rides one of the maharajah's stallions. A man stands to greet us in a field with a generator on his head.

In Jodhpur, Ajai is happy, *very very happy.* And so are we. He is pleased with the drivers' accommodation. We are staying in an airy old guesthouse near the bazaar, with a view across the labyrinth of blue-washed flat roofs towards the gigantic Mehrangarh Fort, its red sandstone ramparts rising sheer out of the 400-foot-high cliff. The guesthouse restaurant is on the roof and the afternoon is warm so we sit outside with Ajai and have a cold beer. The sky is full of soaring swifts. I am quizzing the waiter. He works seven days a week; his family lives seven hours away by bus, he has a baby son. He visits his family once a month, on Sunday.

We go to the bazaar. There is a man selling a broken umbrella. And a man selling pigment, each bright colour heaped into a miraculously tall holy lingam, erect and side-by-side, a rainbow line of phalluses. A man laughs wisely, telling us we are the honey pot and they are the butterflies. And wandering through this landscape in a time apart – ubiquitous, doe-eyed, caramel-coloured, large-humped, unflustered, horns in a crescent moon: the holy cow. In Cow Dimension. Where the rules do not apply.

We buy a street barbecue made out of a cooking-oil tin. A tiny bottle of perfume. A papaya. We step over rag bundles. Past rheumy eyes.

Back on the roof, the waiter intercepts my papaya and whisks it away to peel. Ten minutes later he brings me a roman aqueduct on a plate, a hundred orange moons fanned out, sprinkled with cumin and fresh limes. I thank him with lots of adjectives, he waits, Jonathan thanks him with rupees. The waiter teaches me the Hindu for banana, *kala*; bread, *roti*; view, *drashya*. He writes in my notebook, *app se milana achaha raha* – very nice to meet you. Another waiter refills my coffee, and *dhanybad,* thank you, helps me with my pronunciation. The first waiter tells him to clear the table at the back.

Tonight, Ajai has agreed to eat with us on the roof. We can see the lights of a great palace thirty kilometres away gleaming through the amber dust. The waiter tells us its dining room seats a thousand guests. The sky is full of hunting bats. We are all happy. Ajai is tapping at his mobile phone. Then, with an enormous smile, he passes it to Jonathan and motions him to listen.

There is a confused expression on Jonathan's face. His pupils hop around jerkily like flies. Then he slowly begins to nod. His smile takes on a certain woodenness. But Ajai's smile is broad and brimming. The faint sound coming out of Ajai's phone is of a voice talking very fast. Ajai tells me it is his eldest brother, Hrithik, who is saying hello to Mr Jonathan. The minutes tick past. Jonathan is nodding. His beer grows warm. We watch and wait. Ajai's eyes glitter in rapt expectation. Jonathan says, 'Yes. Yes.' Eventually Jonathan says, 'Nice to talk to you, goodbye,' and passes the phone back to Ajai. He doesn't explain. Which is a bad sign.

'What?' I ask.

'That was Ajai's brother,' he smiles stiffly.

'I know. What did he say?'

He laughs uncomfortably. Our *thali* arrives. Ajai tells us Hrithik is *very highly qualified*. We dip chapatis into the various dishes of aubergine, potatoes, chillies and colourful chutneys. *Enjoy!*

'What did he say?' I ask Jonathan after we've gone to bed.

'Oh God, I don't know.'

'What do you mean you don't know?'

'It was awful.'

'Why?'

Jonathan groans. 'He is coming to the UK. He wants a job in finance. He is *very honoured*. The whole family is honoured that Ajai is our driver. He wants to send me his CV for advice. It's *only a matter of time* before his visa comes through. Then he is able to marry. He wants an English girl. How does he find a good English girl? He knows I will give him good advice. Ajai says we are *good philosophy people*. Then he can take care of his mother and be a *good family head*.'

'He told you all that?'

'Yes.'

'Why does he want to marry an English girl?'

'I have no idea.'

'And where is he planning to stay when he comes to the UK?' I ask warily.

'God knows.'

'Oh, well, just ignore it.'

The next morning Ajai is in a very quiet mood. Did Jonathan not live up to his brother's expectations?

'What's wrong, Ajai?'

He shakes his head.

'What is the matter?'

'Very bad.'

'What is very bad?'

'Very bad news.'

'What news? Is your wife okay?'

'Yes, wife okay. My sister husband made suicide last night.'

'What?'

'Yes.'

'Oh no!'

'Yes. Very bad.'

'Oh dear. I'm sorry, Ajai.'

'Terrible, terrible.'

Ajai explains it is especially bad for his sister because she is newly married and her husband's family will think she has brought bad luck into the house. We say this is ridiculous. He says that is what they will think. They will blame her.

'You must go home, Ajai.'

'No, no. It is for her husband's family to decide.'

'But how is your sister?'

'Very bad.'

'But why did he commit suicide?'

Ajai rocks his head.

'Ajai, if you need to go home, you must go. We can find another driver. We can sort it with your boss.'

'No, no, I am your driver.'

A silent Ajai drives us 200 miles west from Jodhpur to the desert at Jaisalmer; from Jaisalmer, we drop south-east to the Jain temple at Ranakpur with its 1,444 marble pillars, each one carved with a different floral motif. The personable owner of our hotel says he will find us a guide to walk the twenty miles through the forest to the great fort at Kumbhalgarh, while Ajai can drive our bags the fifty-odd kilometres by windy road. He suggests before dinner we walk down to the lake. So we do.

As we head off, a young boy attaches himself to us; with the memory of the girl and the rose we meekly tag along as he leads the way until a shimmering eye of water comes into view.

'Whoa, whoa! Crocodile! Crocodile!' I shout.

I have just seen a massive, man-eating-sized crocodile slide into the lake only a few feet away. I almost trod on it. We watch, amazed and dumbstruck as it swims away, its black outline receding in silver mercury against the red mirrored sky. The boy smiles. *Muggermach,* he teaches us. Now we are all pleased. We had no idea there were crocodiles in the lake. The hotel owner never mentioned it.

'*Muggermach,*' I repeat. 'Very nice word.'

'Crocodile, crocodile,' says the boy.

The boy walks back to the hotel with us for his reward. We

are good friends now. But when we arrive he doesn't want to come in, he wants to wait outside. I insist he comes in. I want to share our excitement and news with the hotel owner. I excitedly tell the owner we have just seen a *muggermach*. He narrows his eyes. He questions the boy. The boy is nervous. The boy replies, his eyes down, his palms flat together, fingers pointing towards his chin. Not the back-patting scenario I'd imagined. Then suddenly the boy prostrates himself on the floor and reaches out to touch the owner's feet. Now I understand why the boy did not want to come in, it is not his place to come in, he is not *supposed* to come in. But we are watching, and so the owner stops the boy. He knows what we will think. Yet we are thinking it nevertheless. The owner tells us we are very fortunate to have seen a crocodile, for he has never seen one. There are only two crocodiles in the lake, one large, and one small. He says you can go to the lake every day for a year and not see one. Outside we give the boy some rupees and he runs away.

The next morning we are up before dawn to meet our guide, and have to step over the four waiters and three hotel staff asleep on the restaurant floor.

Bhima, our tiny forest guide, calls deer *jungly cow, jungly cow*. He points to footprints in the sand, and speaks charmingly in nouns. Just after dawn we hear a commotion of animals and birds alarm-calling. *Leopard, leopard,* Bhima whispers. And there he is, behind a rock. Bhima is delighted, already the day is a success and we've only just begun.

By late afternoon we have emerged from the forest and are

walking through fields where hay is stored high in the trees like gigantic nests so the jungly cows cannot reach it. We see a young woman in a lime-green sari and saffron scarf perched like an exotic bird at the top of a forty-foot tree, its trunk as slender as an arm. No ladder, no companion anywhere. With a machete, she cuts down branches for her goats below.

By the time we arrive at Kumbhalgarh, Ajai's big smile is waiting for us. The mighty walls of the fort stretch for twenty-two miles through the Aravalli hills, wide and strong enough for four elephants to travel abreast.

The subject of Ajai's tip has, in the last few days, grown more urgent in our private conversation. How much? That is the question. Soon we will arrive in Udaipur, our last stop. Ajai has already told us about the driver who was given $250 from a wealthy Canadian which enabled him to rent a shop and start up his own business. I believe we were told it innocently, but it has obviously gone down in driver-tip legend.

'How much?' I ask Jonathan.

'Fifty?'

'What, for two weeks?'

'But that's a lot in India.'

'Not compared to his friend.'

'Two hundred?'

'Two hundred!'

'Well, I don't know.'

I don't know either. We go round and round. Jonathan is reading Rohinton Mistry's *Family Matters* and relates the episode where two men carry an old man home after he took a tumble on the pavement. His stepdaughter debates how much money she should give the men. How far had they carried him? How much did he weigh? Her papa's price in baksheesh is calculated like a sack of wheat. What difference if they were carrying Papa or a gunny of rice? she argues. We laugh. It makes us feel better. Yet we come back to the matter of Ajai's tip, time and time again.

'Seventy-five?'

'Dollars?'

'One hundred?'

'For two weeks?'

Before we give Ajai his tip, or indeed decide on it, we suggest a deal. If he goes home three days early and we catch the train back from Udaipur to Delhi, will he, in return, pick us up from the station, take us to our guesthouse, then take us to Delhi Airport in the morning? It's good? We ask. We think it's very good. Ajai rocks his head from side to side. I am still not getting the side-to-side head rocking, so I don't know whether he thinks this is good, or if there is a problem, or if it is good, but he doesn't like to say it's good, because he likes things the other way around, good for us, not good for him. I say surely he must want to see his family, he must want to see his wife. Yes, he wants to see wife. He rocks his head again.

'We thought you'd *like* to go home, Ajai.'

It seems to have thrown him. He tells us maybe he will get another job and cannot take us to the airport, which forces us to point out that, technically, until just before our flight, he was still supposed to be our driver. He thinks about it. Then agrees. *Enjoy!*

In Udaipur, our room is right on the edge of the lake, where the water laps just below. No more worrying about Ajai's accommodation, for he is speeding back to his wife and mother and bereaved sister and very highly qualified brother, who we are relieved has not rung Jonathan again. As we look across the water we feel doubly lucky – a year ago we would have been looking at eight square kilometres of muddy puddle and lots of rubbish, because for eight years, the famous mirror Lake Pichola disappeared. But in one night, forty inches of rain fell and here it is again. The Venice of the East. A sky mirror for cormorants and storks. A smoky mirror for the big fruit bats that fly from the banyan tree.

At Udaipur train station a porter insists vehemently on carrying both bags. He is dark and thin and wiry. One bag on his head, the other across his shoulder. Short quick steps. Up over the iron bridge to platform eight. Zoom. We run after him, following his thin bare feet across his territory. His millionth crossing. There is a hierarchy of merit, and a pride in the skill of securing a bag against the competition, any weight, any size, then swiftly and strongly delivering it. It is Olympian. I suspect it would be difficult to lure this man away from Train Station World, even for half an hour – he would miss something or somebody, an opportunity, a challenge, an event, a story, a train in, a train out. He finds our seat. Stows our bags. The tip. A massive smile. Hands together in tiny bows. Another crack in my heart.

Our train pulls into Delhi, but where is Ajai? There is no voice coming down the corridor calling *Mr Jonathan, Mr Jonathan*. We've arrived two hours late, but we are sure he will be here, somewhere. And he is. I spot his big smile and clean white shirt at the end of the platform. I'm relieved, because it's a stinking hot day and I'm dirty and sweaty and longing to get to our guesthouse for a shower, and I've been thinking about it for the last five hours on the train. Ajai waves. Then turns to say something to the short plump man in the football shirt and shorts beside him. They walk towards us. Ajai has brought his elder brother, Hrithik. It is a big surprise. They are taking us to the family apartment for lunch. It is all prepared. It is not Ajai telling us this, it is Hrithik, who is sitting where I usually sit, in the front seat.

'You have very good trip I think,' Hrithik says.

'Yes,' Jonathan agrees.

'And Ajai, very good driver I think.'

'Yes, very good,' agrees Jonathan.

Ajai lives a long way from the train station and in the opposite direction from our guesthouse. Tenement blocks loom past with depressing regularity. Hrithik talks all the way, turning in his seat to face Jonathan, his neck twisting like a coil of rope. Hrithik says, 'UK very good practice for Finance Career,' and I zone out, in the airless heat and interminable traffic, as we drive further and further away from our hotel, my legs scrunched together under my bag, the sun drilling into my temples. Ajai's tip shrinking by the minute.

At last, we pull up at the end of a street. Washing lines are strung between the tenement blocks. Kids are batting cricket balls over the washing. Into the washing. Through the washing. They stop to watch as we walk past.

Up five flights of open stairs, and behind the door of Ajai's apartment stands Ajai's mother in a turquoise sari, and Ajai's beautiful wife in a yellow sari. They greet us with shy bows, we shake hands, and they say things we don't understand. Then Hrithik says something and Ajai's wife and mother disappear.

We sit in a small green windowless room which is stiflingly hot, and we listen to Ajai's brother's *UK plans*, which are plentiful, and punctuated by trips to his bedroom to fetch items of clothing which he tries to give to Jonathan.

His jeans.

'No, no, thank you,' Jonathan says. 'Look. I am very tall. I cannot fit, please . . .'

A football shirt.

'No, please! I have no room. I have many shirts. Very kind, but I cannot take.'

His shorts! Hrithik holds them up, *Please take. I give you.* The waist must be forty inches wide.

Jonathan laughs uncomfortably, 'No, please, you keep.'

Another pair of jeans, the legs end just below Jonathan's knees. Jonathan laughs even more uncomfortably. Hrithik wants very much to give Mr Jonathan his trousers. Or his shirt. He fetches more shirts. Nothing will thwart this clothing giveaway. He even offers his shoes.

'You are my uncle,' Hrithik says. 'I have no uncle. Very good uncle, I think.'

Where, oh where have Ajai's wife and mother gone? I ask Ajai. He smiles. They are preparing the food. It is getting hotter and hotter. One hour, two hours. As Hrithik raids his wardrobe there is still no sign of lunch. I slump back, stickily, into the couch, which I now see folds out into their mother's bed. Hrithik is talking about his *Curriculum Vitae*. Ajai is still smiling. Jonathan tells Hrithik that it is very hard in England and sometimes people are not so friendly, that many banks are relocating to India. The future is in India, Jonathan says. But Hrithik is *very focus, very pre-plan*. And then Ajai's wife and mother come in carrying dishes, and I am so glad to see them, and they place different dishes all over the table, but once they have put the dishes down, Hrithik says something and they disappear. My hand almost lurches out to snatch at their saris and drag them back.

'Are your mother and wife not eating with us, Ajai?' I ask desperately.

'No, no. Already eaten,' Hrithik says, wagging his finger.

'Oh, we would love to sit with them. Can they join us?' I look at Ajai beseechingly.

'No, no,' Hrithik rocks his head from side to side, wagging his finger even more vigorously, laughing as if I were crazy.

And so we four are seated as Hrithik decrees, and eat the food Ajai's mother and wife have prepared for us, and they do not reappear until we have finished, when they come back to clear the plates. I rise to help but Hrithik wags his finger again. And only when they have washed the dishes – it must be after four in the afternoon – they return again, and Ajai's lovely wife in her beautiful scarf sits silently, and the mother sits with her hands on her lap, nodding proudly at the ceaseless flow of ambitions from her elder son. Dear Ajai smiles his big happy smile, and Ajai's wife gives me a mosaic cup to hold pencils. We have nothing to give so we take photos of everyone, Hrithik sitting on the high-backed chair in the centre, like a throne, his family standing around him. Hrithik declares Jonathan is his uncle, again, *and very family bonding*, whatever that means, and finally, finally dear Ajai drives us home.

'Oh, oh, oh!' we groan, flumping on the bed. 'Oh!' we moan desperately. 'Oh, oh!' we drum our fists into the pillow. We are laughing and wailing. But we both agree it was not funny. The irony is not lost on us. For the comfortable to be so discomforted.

Next morning we are outside, waiting with our bags for Ajai, as agreed. Our plane leaves in four hours. He will be here any minute, and he is. The white Nissan Sunny turns into the street. And we both groan simultaneously. Hrithik is in the front seat. The envelope bulging with Ajai's tip is sticking out of Jonathan's top pocket, and all I can think is how I'd like to slim it down. And so our last moments in India sink under the weight of our bags on our laps and beneath the sound of Hrithik's plans of getting a *UK job in finance area*, and how Mr Jonathan is uncle to him, and his family will do anything for us, like brother to brother. While outside men at the traffic lights intercept us with trick sleeves which fall down to reveal arm-length rows of self-help books in plastic display pouches: *Seven Habits of Highly*

Effective People, The Feeling Good Handbook, Winning. And though Ajai is driving it is not like it was with the three of us, *telephone kiosk, emancipation, rock climbing, salary, marmalade, padlock, bargain, pass the salt, fizzy pop*, making jokes, laughing, singing along in the billowing dust to Ajai's Indian pop music.

At the airport we hug Ajai. *Goodbye, goodbye, Ajai. Long life and happiness.* Jonathan gives him the envelope. We bow with our hands together. We make our promises. Swap our email addresses. We shake Hrithik's hand.

★

So, how was it? Trevor texts when we get back. Where to begin? It was dusty, buttery, painted, mutilated, price-tagged, red-forted, elephanted, holy, maddening, exhausting, grimy, glorious, shrined, spiced, chock-a-block, billowing, saffroned, turquoised, baffling, burning, perplexing, infuriating, squatted, petalled, full of gods – who eat money – and 800 million freshly laid shits a day. And it isn't finished yet. Because already there is an email waiting in my inbox. From Hrithik.

Dear Mr Jonathan/Ms K

Season Greeting to you. Hope you will be very fine and taking rest after long visit from India.

I am Hrithik, elder brother of your driver Ajai from India who came to receive you at railway station and after that you went with us at our home and also at the time of dropping you at airport I was with Ajai. I believe that you do recognise me now during your recent visit to India with your wife.

I need your help. I just got a mail confirmation from UK National Lottery winning notification from UK. They have contacted me and conveyed please collect your winning funds from their office. They have given me a complete address, contact number with contact person name. Here I need your help, I want that someone visit this place on my behalf as my representative to verify. Then please convey to me so I plan my visit to UK soon to get this money.

I am also attaching two certificates received from them about winning confirmation. So I can deposit require funds for getting Tax Clearance.

Warm Regards,

Hrithik Singh

I open the attachment. If the sketchy upside-down union jacks don't give it away, or the row of cartoon royal crowns, or the dodgy grammar and odd capitalisation, the word STERLINGS certainly does.

I reply.

Dear Hrithik

Your lottery win looks like a fraud. Be careful. Do not give your bank details. Do NOT pay ANY money. If you did not buy a UK National lottery ticket you cannot have won. Only people with UK address can play the UK National lottery. Most scams are based outside the UK. Sorry to disappoint you.

I forward him some websites to check out. He replies.

Dear Mr Jonathan/Ms K

Thank you for effort you made for me to aware such scam. I appreciated you sincere efforts. I am attaching you my resume for re-shape accordingly to UK companies for applying for job.

Be in touch,

Well Regards

Hrithik Singh

I open the attachment. Five dense pages of small type comes up on the screen. Every tick of Hrithik's life, his *Hobbies*, his *Objectives*, his *Outlooks*. I print the pages out, put them on Jonathan's desk. Ten minutes later, another email arrives.

Dear Mr Jonathan/Ms K

One more good news I am getting married in June with Portsmouth girl named Sarah Clark working in Fashion House.

Jonathan you are only contact of mine in UK so I may allow to ask as your younger brother to visit this girl house with your wife for me to check does she really fit for me for my life plan. Hope you will do this for as my uncle do if he had in my life.

Please not tell anything to Ajai for this I wanted to give a big surprise.

Warm Regards

Hrithik Singh

'He wants us to go to Portsmouth and inspect her!' I say.

'I'm not his bloody uncle.'

'You are now.'

'Who is this girl, anyway?'

'How should I know?'

A postcard of a tiger arrives from Ajai.

hello madam, how are you and how are my uncle.

i see tiger in rajisthan. and i got one boy babby is name is Ravi, he is very well. my family very miss to you. now my english are very good so thanu very much. after few days is chrtmas and new year. so enjoy.

Ajai india

Then another email from Hrithik.

Dear Mr Jonathan/Ms K

How is my dearest friend Jonathan, please tell him I really missing him. I am very focus for my future. He will be happy to hear that I am going to marry in June with British National named Sarah Clark who stays in Portsmouth in her own flat. I will get marry in UK then you will be my own guest to bless us. I am self-made person in Metro City life. Please tell me how is she. I do not have Jonathan email id will you give me.

Warmest Regards

Hrithik Singh

'Hurrifik is really missing you, Jonathan.'

'Thanks.'

I am intrigued by the Sarah Clark development. Was she someone he'd met in Delhi, or was this an arranged marriage? Is this an Indian girl with an anglicised name whose parents want to marry her off and have fixed her up with Hrithik? I picture her bent over a sewing machine in a hot warehouse in Portsmouth working a hundred hours a week for a pittance, sending money back to India, waiting for a miracle to save her. Maybe we *should* go and visit her.

Dear Hrithik

What is the situation with Sarah Clark? How did you meet her?

Dear Mr Jonathan/Ms K

I not meet as per yet. I make her contact through yahoo messenger. If you need any information on YOGA please let me know.

Say my hello to Jonathan I am missing him.

Warm regards

Hrithik Singh

'He met her on the internet,' I tell Jonathan.

'Really?'

'Yes. In one of those chat rooms. He hasn't met her in real life.'

'Oh God.'

'More to the point, she's never met him!'

'So why has she agreed to marry him?'

'Haven't a clue. It's not that strange in Indian culture. Maybe she's just desperate to escape her situation. Maybe her parents are forcing her into it? Maybe it's a financial arrangement?'

Dear Madam

As per the recent talk she wants to marry me in June and early plan was of she visiting to India for marry but on my request she has cancelled the programme. Now I am coming in June for marrying her.

She is making in Fashion. Her parents have been expired 2 years before in an car accident as she told me and living in her own flat over the address: 23, Jackson House, Whiteport, Portsmouth. Her number is 0239 284 0330. Dear Madam, Request to you please check her fact she has given me if that fact is correct then I'll decide to marry her.

Say my hello to Jonathan I am missing him

Warm regards

Hrithik Singh

'Her parents have been killed in a car crash, apparently,' I tell Jonathan.

'What? Both of them?' Jonathan says.

'That's what he says.'

It all sounds very odd. I now have a firm image of a lonely, orphan Indian girl cutting out patterns all day. Then I picture a plump bespectacled one, quite a bit older . . . I'm not sure if I believe the parents-killed-in-car-crash thing, but I am becoming more and more curious.

Dear Hrithik

How did you make your initial contact, what is Yahoo Messenger?

Dear Mr Jonathan/Ms K

friendsabroad.com

Dear Hrithik

What financial arrangements have been discussed? Are you paying an introductory fee or giving your bank details? What else do you know about Sarah Clark?

Dear Madam

I was told there are special marriage office and all this functions will be costing around only 100 pounds. We have not discuss any financial arrangements. Even not known about introductory fee. I make her contact through yahoo messanger as explan. Request to you please guide me what is process of getting marry in UK.

I looking forward seeing with my uncle as visit with a brother.

Hrithik Singh

'I'm fed up with this,' Jonathan says.

Dear Hrithik

We think it is better she visits you in India before you both decide. Arranged marriage is not our custom here. The custom here is love marriage.

Dear Mr Jonathan/Ms K

Firstly, Infact, sorry you have understood wrong me in my communication. She proposed me for this marriage, She loves me very much i also loves her an this is not arranged marriage this will be a love marriage and will happen in the month of May in England with your custom (her photo attached for you) so you will see what all is. Request you please now checking process of getting marry in UK.

Warm regards

Hrithik Singh

Well, if I'm going to call this Sarah Clark (yes, I'm intrigued enough to call her), I'd quite like to know what she looks like. I'm *dying* to know what she looks like. My cursor hovers over the photo attachment. I hold my breath as I click.

1 Attachment, 350.KB

Sarah, bsmp.

With our (pre-broadband) slow internet speed, the 350 KB file takes a few moments to download. Then the photograph comes up on the screen . . .

THE LAST THING

It is Sunday, 11 September to be precise (having consulted the campervan diary), and Jonathan and I and our two dogs, Frida and Jessie, are driving west across France in our campervan. We have been visiting some friends in Aubais near the Camargue, who run painting holidays for people who want to paint horses. For years I have been seduced by photographs of the wild white stallions of the Camargue charging through water and spray, but I had no idea how searingly hot it can get in this part of France, so we are now heading west to higher ground where we can camp under shady poplars and find cool rivers to swim in. And as we are driving along listening to Bill Callahan singing 'One Fine Morning' we have an idea. A dangerous idea. To return to a place, a very special place, a place locked into our hearts as the idyllic impossibly sublime heaven-on-earth best camping spot we have ever found, on the best camping holiday we have ever had, where everything, *everything* went RIGHT. Uh-oh.

'Should we?' I ask Jonathan.

'Why shouldn't we?' he replies, nonplussed.

'Well, you know . . .'

But he doesn't really. He seems a bit cavalier, a bit too trusting, not *au fait* with the ways of the world. Sod's world. Because I am thinking this could be courting disappointment. Big time. And yet . . . it was the most wonderful place. Dare we? Or should we leave it there untarnished in our memories, pure and perfect and safe, to see us into our dotage. But the name has been uttered, and the elemental force and the folly of desire to taste Arcadia once more has been unleashed; the tight spiral of good sense is already unspiralling, and as we both know, it is unstoppable now. That tiny village in the Lot Valley beside its cool clear tributary nestled under its limestone cliff, where the swallows wheeled in the evening's last blushed rays of the day's sun which flooded the rock face into a glowing opalescent shell pink. Oh! And the perfect camping spot, *our* spot, beside the cool running river, under the tall poplars with their rattling leaves, just a flower meadow away from the medieval village with its clock tower and honeyed-stone buildings huddled together, entwined by grape vines over patios where chickens scratched in the dry dust. And the boulangerie that baked its bread from flour ground in the mill across the street, which still rolled its great wheel in the cool clear river, beside the swans' nests and the hidden holes of king-fishers.

And more! Only the best, authentic, real French traditional restaurant in the world (for us anyway), just as a French village restaurant would be in your wildest dreams. But it wasn't in our dreams, it was impossibly lovely, with a trained grapevine over the sun-drenched patio, which let the sun cascade through like flickering minnows and was home to an avian world of chattering sparrows who hopped about and chirruped and stole crumbs off the tables. And the restaurant was full of French people, which was a good sign, and a scattering of pilgrims, for the village was on the Santiago route of Coquille St Jacques. It was run by an elderly sister and her elderly brother, and had been in the family through generations and hardly changed, and just outside the restaurant, the elderly brother parked his old Citroën Traction Avant – an antique Citroën with gleaming paint and polished chrome, and sweeping wheel arches like giant eyebrows, on whose walnut dashboard he kept an old French magazine dated 1921. And next to his antique Citroën he parked an ancient scooter and sometimes an old bicycle because he was passionate about old vehicles.

What a scene. It looked heavenly and it was heaven, and Frida and Jessie were allowed to sit under the table and watch the sparrows hop about. And even better, there was no menu, which hooray meant you didn't have to worry about choosing the *wrong* thing. We were just brought course after course of French things on plates, and a basket of homemade bread made from the village-milled flour, which was put on your table with a pitcher of wine, and everyone was given the same thing, starting with a cold platter of charcuterie and spears of freshly picked asparagus, and then it was grilled aubergines and peppers, followed by slow-cooked lamb stew with caramelised onions and garlic and, and, and sautéed potatoes, and then a homemade clafoutis of plums, oh, oh, and then a yard of cheeses of different shapes and sizes and smells and textures, which of course was when Jonathan ordered the marc, which lit up his reddening face, brighter and redder, as we slid back into our chairs saying, right now, right here, this must be the best place in the whole world and we are in heaven. We remember it so well. Those Canadian pilgrims who told us they had read about this very place in *American Gourmet* twenty years ago and had always wanted to come and now they were here, and how amazed they were that it was everything they'd read and dreamed about. And we oohed and ahhed and chinked our glasses as sparrow wings whirred above.

And then the river, oh the river! Rowing upstream in our inflatable Canadian canoe (which carries all four of us and a picnic) as far as we could, then gliding back along its secret winding world through tunnels of trees, past ducks and coots, keeping an eye out for roosting bats under the old stone bridges, past ancient cave dwellings built into the high rocks. We have held it in our memory, with its smells and sounds. Frida in the front, leaning on my leg, two paws on the gunnels, literally shivering with excitement as red squirrels leapt from branch to branch, her eyes bright, her ears twitching, listening acutely to the lapping and quacking and flapping of creatures of the rivery world. The iridescent flash of a kingfisher across our wake, its peeping cry. Kingfisher, *martin-pêcheur*. Perched in the shadows on an overhanging branch, we hold it in our mind's eye with *its* eye intent on a glimmering shadow in the water. The music of the water remains with us, its ballet of aqua light, its quivering mercury skin, its mysterious dark pools. And, ah yes, the day we met some walkers with a donkey in the village square, who took us with them on their afternoon hike into the hills along the narrow goat paths where mountain oaks dropped acorns and wild boar foraged; how we walked along together with that natural ease of travelling strangers, until we found a shepherd's stone shelter where we shared their homemade plum cake and plum cognac.

Oh, yes, that holiday was etched indelibly, every detail, every nuance, almost otherworldly. The holiday where everything blossomed into more than itself. The sun shone, the swallows wheeled, the kingfishers fished, we even spotted an otter swimming across the river then disappearing into its holt. We rowed after its trail and peered into the dark wet riverine hole, amazed. Each morning I swam through the first fallen leaves and each evening we sat on our camp chairs, with our cold rosé and salted cashews, watching the swallows in thermal updrafts, as the sun sank into its pinks and violets, and the yellow sulphur lights of the huddled village came on one by one illuminating the clock tower, warming the stone as if lit by fire, as if from another time. It was *impossibly* romantic.

*

We drive along remembering, the road rumbling beneath our tyres, Bill Callahan singing 'Drover'. We must be mad. Could we *really* countenance going back?

Jonathan wants to know what we are going to do, because if we *are* going, we need to turn off the motorway very soon. But the closer we come to the turn-off, the bigger the dilemma becomes. It is almost like testing a sacred law, for surely we must safeguard the memory and leave it in its perfect box? Yet here we are, greedily wanting more. I am reading the map, my head and heart in combat, because there is still time to back out now, but if we *are* going, we will need to turn off in about ten minutes. But of course I know. We both know. The spell has been invoked. And ten minutes later the indicator light is flicking and we have left the motorway. And while I am full of excitement I am also full of dread.

With each mile the expectation increases, as does the dread. I go through every scenario. Out loud. Jonathan silently driving. It is foolhardy. The campsite will be closed. The weather will be terrible. There will be a new building development in the village with cement mixers and dumper trucks. The road will be being dug up and tarmac lorries will be coming and going. There will be hunting dogs barking relentlessly in a large cage on the hill. There will be an electric storm bringing down all the power lines, so loud generators will be set up chugging out noise and fumes all day. Madame and her elderly brother will not be running the restaurant, they will have retired . . . or worse. What else will be amiss? I rack my brains for every scenario, either to prepare myself or – and I am not sure which is more accurate here – in the superstitious belief that by naming it, it can never happen.

Everything I can think of. Almost like a game. Like I-spy.

'We don't *have* to go,' Jonathan says.

But we do. And I lather myself up into intestinal knots. One hour, two hours, well on the way. Too late to turn back now. Road signs begin to indicate our proximity. We are entering the terrain. We drive on, almost silent. By now I am convinced that if the campsite *is* still there, our spot will definitely be taken by campers from hell, with loud thumping music and shouting all night, or wild Italian schoolchildren, or thirty German bikers, or a stag party of English louts. Tomorrow there will be a mistral blowing. And worst of all, the restaurant will be shut. Fools are we to think anything could ever live up to that hallowed time.

And now we have turned onto the road that runs along the actual valley itself. And the sun is shining. Fifteen kilometres to go. I am holding my heart in my mouth, I've almost stopped breathing. Really, my nervousness is ridiculous. Closer and closer. Past each bridge, past each village. I can hardly speak. I know around this next bend will be the village sign. My eyes are craning out. And there it is! And it looks surprisingly just like the village I remember. I can see the tops of the poplar trees of the campground. And the camp sign . . . it is there, and yes, it is open! And I can already see *there is no one in our favourite spot*! I am like a child, impatient to get in there and grab it, thinking at any moment someone else might sneak in front of us and get there first.

We pull up outside the little office reception, ratchet the handbrake on, and go in. I am almost dancing on the spot. The man in reception is watching rugby. Jonathan jokes with him, something about rugby, ho, ho. Come on, come on. It takes all my willpower not to run down to the river and stand childishly on our pitch marking it out as bagged territory. And we hand in our Irish passports, proud of the Éire and the gold harp, as if it has anything to do with us, not English, no, no. And we fill in the form and look out the window to check the registration of the van, and then, at last, we hop back into the campervan and cheer and drive down to our spot. We park between the two poplars facing west for the last rays of sun, making a meal as usual about backing into the *exact* right spot. We unpack our camp chairs, click them out, slot the camp table together. Haul the inflatable canoe off the roof rack. Chain our bikes to the tree. Feed the dogs. And then we all go down to the river for a christening swim, and it is as beautiful as I remember, and the four of us slither in, Frida following me and Jessie swimming after a stick, and we have it all to ourselves and everything is dreamy and sublime, the water tea-coloured, and every now and again the muscled back of a fish is caught by a shaft of sun. The dogs roll in the grass, the bottle of rosé and salted cashews are on the camp table, the swallows wheel in front of the cliff, and we nervously toast the evening and the village and the *right* decision to return, as slowly the lights come on, still sulphur yellow, and the village glows like honey in front of us. No roadworks. No generator. No howling chasse dogs. No development. No cranes. No noisy neighbours. For tonight ... The fear, of course, unspoken, is that it will be *the restaurant* that disappoints.

In the morning, after my swim, during which I stubbed my

toe on a submerged log thinking the river deeper in my normal getting-in place than it turned out to be, we meander across the flowery meadow to the village with our shopping bag. The mill is still working, the boulangerie still open, the shop is still there. The boucherie van is in its normal position. Nervously we cross the road for our first view of the restaurant. And it is still there! And it is open! And the Citroën Traction Avant is parked outside. With the 1921 magazine on the dashboard. And we bound up the steps and Madame is there, and we smile madly and book a table for lunch under the vines. And we skip back home to our camp with our shopping bags full of wine and cashews and cheese and apricots, and blow up the canoe. Silly to doubt, to be so fatalistic. What is *wrong* with me? Expecting the dark hand of fate at every turn. *Everything* is fine. Everything is dandy. It is sunny and I get out my watercolours and float turquoise pigment in watery blobs onto blank postcards; and then we walk to the restaurant, which is as full as ever with French people and pilgrims, the vines full of sparrows, and the sun filters through, flickering like a Renoir onto the tables, and we have charcuterie with melon, a pitcher of rosé, a basket of homemade bread, and then comes entrecôte with garlic and French fries, and then a platter of cheese, and then poire au chocolat and some chocolate almond things and creamy things. Delicious and heavenly, and Frida and Jessie are complimented on their good behaviour, and how lucky, we say we are, a*gain*.

And we are a bit tipsy with the wine and the sun when after lunch we haul the canoe down to the river, because we have forgotten the right place to get in and somehow have chosen a muddy place full of sticks and logs which I don't remember from before, and Frida gets stuck in some mud, and the canoe gets stuck, but we push it out and row down past the camp and into the tunnel of trees. But we are too sleepy to row far, so we drift back and decide *tomorrow* will be the day of The Big Canoe Adventure. Today will be the sleeping day. So we haul the canoe out, and we watch the swallows circle, and snooze as the sun goes down.

The next morning, a little later than my planned eight o'clock before-breakfast swim, I pad down to the river bank, and I stop. And I stare. I stare, because the bank is there, the trees are there, but the river . . . is gone. The river isn't there. And I can't compute it. And it isn't possible. But it is possible. Because that is what is front of my eyes. Rather, not in front of my eyes. I stare, discombobulated. When I say there is no river, I mean that there is no river water, nothing flowing, just a few pools in a landscape of mud and branches and stones and exposed logs. It is now a slick worm-channel of ex-river, its path is still there all right, but not the river itself. This was not a stream that could just evaporate in the sun, it was a tributary of the Lot, a proper river, thirty feet across. With fish in it. I stand and stare. I blink. It is impossible.

All that cool flowing earth water, with its earth smells and earth-cold velvet caresses, gone? I look away and look back. It is still gone. And I am still in the same place staring. I don't know what to do. Slowly, I turn, and then leadenly make my way back to the campervan. I stand in the door.

'What's the matter?' Jonathan wants to know.

I don't bother to explain. 'Come with me,' I say.

We both walk down to the river bank. Even now I am hoping it isn't true. We cannot work it out and we can hardly believe it. You really had to see it with your own eyes. It almost feels as if I have caused it with my ridiculous worrying. It is a visitation from the serve-you-right River-Draining God. No canoeing today, no finger trailing in the water's wake. No Frida quaking at red squirrels leaping from branch to branch. No kingfisher flash. Breakfast is hardly appealing, I cannot do anything until we have got to the bottom of this. We trudge listlessly along the no river to the boulangerie. We ask.

The mayor (it's always the mayor in France) has drained the river to fix the weir and barrage where the fast water channel of the mill race has undermined it. It has been years in the planning and this is the week. I was unaware that a river can be disappeared in such an alarmingly short amount of time – its flow, its pace – but somehow it has been. Of course, there is nothing we can do about it – this week, the week of our return, out of all the weeks in the last four years, is *the* week of the barrage repairs, and there will be no river for the entire duration of our stay. The river is off. It has been redirected, like a detour, to God knows where, and I have no idea what the kingfishers do, what the otter does, what the fish do. But I know this is the holiday that will always be remembered for *the last thing* one could possibly ever have imagined, the *impossible* thing, the river that vanished. In the campervan diary I draw a scratchy black ink sketch of our campervan packed up and ready to leave. And off we go.

ACKNOWLEDGEMENTS

Thank you to my friend and agent, the incomparable Patrick Walsh, whose explosive bellowing laugh I've been fortunate to hear on so many occasions during the course of this book, and whose vast reserves of wisdom, good humour and generosity never cease to amaze me.

I am lucky to have the judicious Simon Thorogood as my editor, and thank him for his thoughtfulness, guidance and care. Thank you to the astonishing hawk-eyed Leila Cruickshank, my copyeditor. Thanks also to Vicki Rutherford. Enormous gratitude to the very wonderful Lucy Zhou. And to Jamie Byng and the good ship Canongate for welcoming me on board. Thanks to Will Atkins for editorial comments. To John Ash for everything. To Patrick Harpur. To Jamie Telford and Jane Gifford for a contribution towards the camel. To Michael Neill, Sam Neill, Ian Wilks, Jocelyn Pook, Graeme Miller, Trevor Stuart, Adam Dant and Ned Holland. My thanks (and apologies) to all witting and unwitting participants in these tales.

Most of all, thank you to Jonathan Thomson, fall guy, semi-patient husband, best friend.